IMAGES
of America

MOUNT WASHINGTON
AND DUQUESNE HEIGHTS

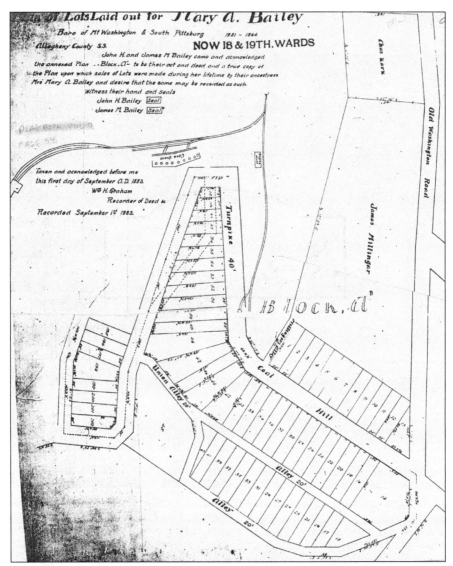

Mary Ann Bailey was the daughter of Jacob Beltzhoover and granddaughter of Melchor Beltzhoover, who came to Pittsburgh in the late 1700s. Mary Ann married Francis Bailey and they had six children, two of whom were notable in Mount Washington: Judge John H. Bailey and James Madison Bailey. The brothers had this map drawn in 1883 to represent the original subdivision laid out by their mother between the years 1851 and 1864. It is farm No. 4 in the Plan of Tracts laid out in 1784 within the Pittsburgh Manor south of Coal Hill. This area's importance lies in its history of providing the transport of coal to the foundries and glass works along the Monongahela River. (Courtesy of Michael Liss.)

On the cover: To validate the authenticity of the picture, a search was done of the 1890–1895 city directories that are housed in the Historical Society of Western Pennsylvania. Mary Reed did indeed have a boarding house on Southern Avenue in the late 1800s. Judge Sarah Soffel referenced the boarding house in an article in the *Mount Washington News* in 1954. Soffel was the first woman judge in Pennsylvania and a lifelong resident of Mount Washington. (Courtesy of Lois Knell.)

IMAGES
of America

MOUNT WASHINGTON
AND DUQUESNE HEIGHTS

Nancy J. Kimmerle Beck

ARCADIA
PUBLISHING

Published by Arcadia Publishing
Charleston, South Carolina

Library of Congress Catalog Card Number: 2006935067

For all general information contact Arcadia Publishing at:
Telephone 843-853-2070
Fax 843-853-0044
E-mail sales@arcadiapublishing.com
For customer service and orders:
Toll-Free 1-888-313-2665

Visit us on the Internet at www.arcadiapublishing.com

CONTENTS

ACKNOWLEDGMENTS

The following individuals contributed greatly to the completion of this book. Michael Liss, David Vater, Lois Knell, Cel Mazzarini, and Marion Streiff from the Mount Washington Branch of the Carnegie Library were kind enough to attend two meetings where they offered information, pictures, and wise counsel. They encouraged me to continue with the task and were available to help with questions about historical accuracy. Sr. Mary Bride O'Malley, the St. Mary of the Mount alumni director, allowed me to use photographs from her collection. Ethan Raup, director of the Mount Washington Community Development Corporation, and Greg Panza, the program director, offered assistance and provided some current photographs of the city. Miriam Meislik, the archivist from the University of Pittsburgh Digital Library was helpful in my search for images from the past. Lisa Lazar and Lauren Zabelski from the Historical Society of Western Pennsylvania made exceptions in providing images, and Gilbert Pietrzak from the Pennsylvania Department of the Carnegie Library helped with images. For help with computer problems and disk burning, I thank Leonard Shapiro. I must thank those people who trusted me with their treasured photographs, many of which are irreplaceable. Without their willingness to share pictures and information about their homes, their lives, and their ancestors, this book could not have been made.

Every effort has been made to obtain correct factual information and to acknowledge all contributors to this project.

INTRODUCTION

Brendan Gill, a columnist in the *New Yorker* wrote on January 9, 1989, "If Pittsburgh were situated somewhere in the heart of Europe, tourists would eagerly journey hundreds of miles out of their way to visit it. Its setting is spectacular, between high bluffs, where the Monongahela River and the Allegheny River meet to form the Ohio."

Later, words were not so kind. Known as the "smoky city," disparaging words were commonplace; even today, the name lingers. Yet, Pittsburghers know differently. The "high bluff" spoken of by Gill is comprised of Mount Washington and Duquesne Heights, two neighborhoods with a vast amount of history, contributing greatly to the picture of Pittsburgh.

Early travelers can best describe Mount Washington and Duquesne Heights. One traveler remarked on the dwellings seen on the side of the hill and the remarkable minerals found on the surface such as marble, slate, and coal. The marble was bluish in color and harder than common limestone. Above the marble was coarse slate and then coal. The coal found here was all the more remarkable because of its closeness to the surface. This bed of coal was 10-to-12 feet thick and extended over the whole hill. And thus, it became known as Coal Hill.

Another traveler described the hill: "A hundred years ago the hills rose from the water's edge to the height of a mountain, with two or three puny houses squeezed in between it and the river. On its summit stood a farmhouse and barn of Major Kirkpatrick. The barn was burned down by the heroes of the Whiskey Rebellion and the resulting fire threw a light so bright over the city that one might see to pick up a pin."

Alas, no one commemorates the finder of coal on Coal Hill. For it is due to his discovery that industries such as steel mills and glass factories flourished. The unknown hero is a British soldier from the garrison at Fort Pitt who scraped away the shale from the hillside and dug out a portion of it which he loaded on his canoe, paddled across the river, and kindled the fire to warm his dreary barracks. Vast coal reserves were to spell riches for hundreds and a livelihood for thousands. Edward Ward, leader of the first white settlers, opened the first coal pit on the hill, somewhere between what is now the Fort Pitt Bridge and the West End Bridge. The first glass factory was established by James O'Hara at the base of Duquesne Heights and was fed by the coal from Ward's mine. Other mines followed quickly, and it is recorded that the first coal mined was in 1760. The time was right because it was two years after the British had driven the French from Fort Duquesne. The first residents were English, Scotch-Irish, and Welsh, who worked in the glass factories. The Germans followed. Mount Washington and the South Side were included in a 3,000-acre royal grant to Maj. John Ormsby in 1770 for his service in the French and Indian War. As industries thrived, more and more workers were required. And it is the workers and their families that are chronicled in this book. It was their lives, their endeavors, and their faith that pulled them through.

One

THE CHALLENGE
OF HILLS

The story of Mount Washington is the quest to conquer its formidable heights. Although soldiers from Fort Pitt discovered coal here as early as 1754, residential development did not occur for another 120 years. This was due to the difficulty of negotiating its steep face and the inconvenience of traveling around the backside of the hill in pre-automobile days. During those early years, coal mining and its related activity defined the hill. In fact, the coal seam was so important that its discovery directly contributed to the industrial development of Pittsburgh and the mount became known as Coal Hill. Coal from Mount Washington, the proximity of the rivers, and the flats at the foot of the hill provided a natural setting for manufacturing.

One of the first attempts to conquer the mount was the invention of the inclined plane to bring coal downhill to the factories. This unique conveyance utilized a descending coal-filled hopper to pull up an empty hopper by means of a shared cable. Equipping the inclines with steam power allowed goods and passengers to now be brought uphill as well as downhill. The development of motorized inclined planes in the 1870s paved the way for residential expansion on Mount Washington.

Early settlement had consisted mainly of miners, their families, and a few farmers. When the coal seam was exhausted on the hill and the cramped South Side could no longer provide space for housing, the topography of the hilltop underwent a dramatic change as mining companies and farmers subdivided and sold their land for residential development. Eventually, three passenger inclines were constructed on Mount Washington and Duquesne Heights to accommodate the real estate boom. Two of these also provided freight service, which could haul an entire wagon filled with building materials to satisfy the voracious demand for housing.

This is an early view of the hardships suffered by early coal miners and their families. Sketched by H. Fenn for the magazine *Early Saturday*, it depicts family life on Coal Hill and gives an indication of how coal was transported up and down the hill. "Pittsburgh is not a beautiful city," wrote William Glazier in the late 19th century. How could it be possible when the hills were alive with coal, coal miners, and dust? There was an unchanging heavy pall of smoke unrivaled in the world, but Pittsburgh's inhabitants did not seem to mind. After all, it provided their livelihood. (Courtesy of the Pennsylvania Department, Pittsburgh Photographic Library, Carnegie Library, Pittsburgh.)

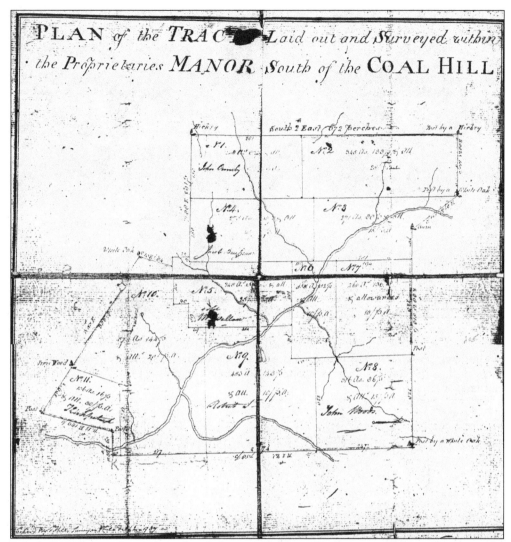

Dated 1787, this is the earliest detailed map of Mount Washington. William Penn was the proprietor of Penn's Woods until the Revolutionary War. As a British citizen, he was deprived of his holdings in Pennsylvania. However, he was allowed to keep certain tracts known as manors. The Manor of Pittsburgh consisted mostly of the downtown area, but included Beechview, Brookline, Mount Washington, Banksville, and West Liberty. Maj. John Ormsby, awarded many acres for his service at Fort Pitt, purchased farm No. 1 in 1791. William Boggs purchased No. 2, No. 3, and No. 6 in 1793, 1794, and 1803, respectively. Jacob Bausman purchased No. 4 and later sold it to Melchor Beltzhoover. George Wallace, a judge, purchased No. 5, but in 1797, he sold 180 acres to William Boggs. Archibald McDermott purchased No. 7. John Woods purchased farm No. 8, and Robert Snodgrass bought farm No. 9 in 1774. Abraham Kirkpatrick bought No. 10 in 1794. No. 11 was presented to Kirkpatrick as a commission for his military service. Along with No. 10, Kirkpatrick owned all of the front part of Mount Washington.

As seen from Mount Washington in 1898, the Smithfield Street Bridge took traffic into and out of downtown Pittsburgh. It crossed the Monongahela River at the base of Mount Washington. A resident of Sycamore Street remembers that in the early 1900s there was a large clock at the entry to the bridge. She checked it every morning to make sure that she was not late for school.

This is an early view of the Monogahela Incline. The buildings on the crest are in Mount Washington. Notice that there are two sets of tracks. One set is for the incline that carried horses and buggies. The sign at the top says New Incline.

Imagine laboring for hours in a black and dusty coal mine or in a hot and stifling glass factory and then having to trudge up these winding and crooked steps to get home. Called the Indian Trail, this path was one of the sophisticated networks of trails originally created by Native Americans—the Delaware, the Shawnee, Seneca, or Iroquois—who lived here. Native Americans made this circuitous and meandering path probably to get to the river for water. Prior to 1700, this region was a vast wilderness inhabited by wild animals and wandering bands of Native Americans. Coal miners and glass workers benefited from the work of these early inhabitants. (Courtesy of the Pittsburgh City Photographer Collection, Archives Service Center, University of Pittsburgh.)

Walkers going down the lengthy Duquesne Heights steps into the city had a long time to view the city and the rivers. In the far distance the Cathedral of Learning stands out on the horizon. The scene is spectacular: high bluffs with the rivers in between. Today, tourists and pleasure-seekers would relish the experience of climbing the Indian Trails. (Courtesy of the Pittsburgh City Photographer Collection, Archives Service Center, University of Pittsburgh.)

The Duquesne Heights Incline hovers over a small section of the boardwalk of the Indian Trail steps. The picture was taken from atop the North Pole Cold Storage Plant in 1935. It is hoped that the Indian Trail steps may be recreated. (Courtesy of the Pittsburgh City Photographer Collection, Archives Service Center, University of Pittsburgh.)

Little boys, mothers, and residents watch as workmen prepare Excelsior Street for paving. July 7, 1909, was not that long ago, but many streets in Mount Washington and Duquesne Heights were just then being paved. (Courtesy of the Pittsburgh City Photographer Collection, Archives Service Center, University of Pittsburgh.)

14

Curious neighborhood boys lounge on the fence to make sure that the work is done properly. Sewer repairs were in process at the bottom of Lelia Street on August 20, 1925. The railroad tracks are behind the bushes and billboard advertising dots the hillside. Workmen's tools are scattered near the pit. (Courtesy of the Pittsburgh City Photographer Collection, Archives Service Center, University of Pittsburgh.)

From the front of 225 Lelia Street looking east, workers are making improvements to the roadway. Trees were removed and the horses pull a wagonload of what appears to be paving blocks. The large square structure on the right is a steam shovel from the Thaw Steam Shovel Company. The date is August 12, 1925, and the roads were almost always impossible for automobiles due to mud and nearly vertical streets. Under these conditions, horses were a blessing. (Courtesy of the Pittsburgh City Photographer Collection, Archives Service Center, University of Pittsburgh.)

Early in the 1900s, streets remained unpaved. Pictured is Kirkpatrick Street in 1910. Unpaved streets grew into quagmires when rain or snow came, which was often in Pittsburgh. They were hardly usable for residents, much less the postman or deliverymen. The real danger was when the refuse could not be collected. (Courtesy of the Library and Archives Division, Historical Society of Western Pennsylvania, Pittsburgh.)

The P. J. McArdle Roadway, after extensive preparation, was finally paved in 1928. Previously named the Mount Washington Roadway, it was renamed to honor Peter J. McArdle who lived on Bigham Street. He was elected to the Pittsburgh City Council in 1911 where he served for 27 years and was a member of the city planning commission when the Mount Washington Roadway improvements were discussed. (Courtesy of the Pittsburgh City Photographer Collection, Archives Service Center, University of Pittsburgh.)

Pictured are the Liberty Tunnels, or the tubes, as they were commonly called. Finished in 1924, they are pictured here in August 1926. An automobile is seen heading toward the Mount Washington Roadway. Notice that there is a house on the right side of the road. Two years later, in 1928, the P. J. McArdle Roadway would be built farther to the left and up the steep part of the hill. (Courtesy of the Pittsburgh City Photographer Collection, Archives Service Center, University of Pittsburgh.)

Wyoming Street is being repaved with cobblestones in July 1910. Streetcar tracks run along this street. What a bumpy ride it must have been for the horse and wagon that was waiting by the lumberyard on the left. The name on the building was Jas Richie and Son. A fire on July 4, 1920, thought to have been a misdirected skyrocket, destroyed the old Richie Lumber Company yard and a number of houses. The Church League played a benefit baseball game at Olympia Park for the victims of the fire. (Courtesy of the Pittsburgh City Photographer Collection, Archives Service Center, University of Pittsburgh.)

Pictured is the south portal of the Mount Washington trolley tunnel as it looked in 1910. The tracks on the right were for trolleys coming from Knoxville and some sections of the mount. The tracks on the left served the South Hills areas of Beechview, Dormont, Mount Lebanon, and Brookline. All streetcars traveled under Mount Washington to arrive in the downtown area of the city. (Courtesy of the Pittsburgh City Photographer Collection, Archives Service Center, University of Pittsburgh.)

Pictured is a view of the footbridge leading to the Duquesne Incline from West Carson Street. The raised bridge provided safety for incline users to get across Carson Street. The Thorofare Store advertises Green Stamps as a premium. (Courtesy of the Pittsburgh City Photographer Collection, Archives Service Center, University of Pittsburgh.)

Two

THE CITY GROWS

One way to learn about the growth of the city is to pay attention to the recollections of old time residents. Two such residents were Judge Sarah Soffel and Herbert Steinbrink. Soffel's musings were recorded in the *Mount Washington News* in August 1954. Born on October 26, 1886, and a lifelong resident, Soffel remembered flames from blast furnaces "leaping to the heavens" from the furnaces at the bottom of the hill. Grandview Avenue was there as long as she lived, but there were no fancy lights as she looked over the hill. Her father, Jacob Soffel, built the house where she lived as a child. Across the street from her house on Southern Avenue was a lumberyard and down the street was a boarding house run by Mary Reed. There was no big industry; only small businesses such as Billy Golden who sold oil lamps, Mr. Engle who sold harnesses, Samuel Discher who built the Monongahela Incline, and Mr. Brethauer who owned a grocery store. In her day, Mount Washington was a wooded area with open land. The buildings came later.

As recorded by S. Trevor Hadley, Herbert Steinbrink, who was born on December 17, 1898, recalled that when his family moved to Mount Washington, Grandview Avenue was not yet paved, it was very narrow, and had room for only one vehicle. His grandfather built about five houses in Mount Washington, including one for his family, which was located where P. J. McArdle Roadway started down the hill. It had a glass enclosure in the back, which overlooked the city. "That view is priceless today," he said, "but then they were so used to it that they got sick of looking at it." However, in an unexpected windstorm, the house was damaged and his mother refused to live there any longer.

The town was indeed growing. Streets were being paved, transportation was increasing, more people were moving up the hill due to the inclines, churches were being built, and communities were developing. More and more businesses were serving the residents.

Boardwalks were the only way to avoid the mud and muck that was ever present on Lelia Street after rain or snow. This picture was taken on April 23,1916, when ladies still wore ankle length dresses. However, progress was being made with streetlights and telegraph poles.

This picture of Manor Street was taken to show the condition of the road; possibly because a proposed location for the Knox school was down the street. The date was June 8, 1931. (Courtesy of the Pittsburgh City Photographer Collection, Archives Service Center, University of Pittsburgh.)

Workmen are preparing Boggs Avenue for a new pipeline, restricting traffic to one side of the road. Collyer's Realty is on the left, halfway up the street, as identified by its sign. The white building in the distance was Fuh's Restaurant. It was once a much-loved restaurant, but is now a laundromat. (Courtesy of the Pittsburgh City Photographer Collection, Archives Service Center, University of Pittsburgh.)

Clothes hanging on the line with clothes poles holding up the line seem to be in danger of getting dirty, considering that the hillside is so close. It appears that a car was junked on the hillside. It is June 8, 1931, and the hillside is near the proposed extension of the Mount Washington Roadway extension. (Courtesy of the Pittsburgh City Photographer Collection, Archives Service Center, University of Pittsburgh.)

Looking west from 1304 Grandview Avenue are two girls waiting patiently for the Belgian block to be laid on their street. The paving was part of the Road Improvement Project of Mount Washington. (Courtesy of the Pittsburgh City Photographer Collection, Archives Service Center, University of Pittsburgh.)

On June 13, 1928, Grandview Avenue had stacks of Belgian block in preparation for paving the street. Seen from 1315 Grandview Avenue, a streetcar gets a little assistance at the end of the road. Two businesses are at the left; one is a barbershop with the traditional barbershop pole. (Courtesy of the Pittsburgh City Photographer Collection, Archives Service Center, University of Pittsburgh.)

Two boys stand on Grandview Avenue at the intersection of Oneida Street on October 8, 1907. No traffic is in sight. It seems that the road is being prepared for paving. When the streetcar tracks end as is seen here, the motorman moves to the other end of the car and reverses direction. (Courtesy of the Pittsburgh City Photographer Collection, Archives Service Center, University of Pittsburgh.)

A grocery store sits on unpaved Virginia Avenue in 1926. Some customers may have had to traverse the muddy road and possibly duck traffic because the boardwalk was only on one side of the road. A dog and his mistress stand on the porch of the store. (Courtesy of the Pittsburgh City Photographer Collection, Archives Service Center, University of Pittsburgh.)

Could these workmen standing in a row in the ditch be paving Paul Street on June 23, 1910? It is likely because there is so much debris on the side of the road. The styles of workmen's hats have changed quite a bit since then. (Courtesy of the Pittsburgh City Photographer Collection, Archives Service Center, University of Pittsburgh.)

As Paul Street was being paved in 1910, residents in the home at the right requested retaining walls. It does not look like they got them. A workman stands next to the sign at the left. (Courtesy of the Pittsburgh City Photographer Collection, Archives Service Center, University of Pittsburgh.)

William Street, one block down from Bailey Avenue, had sidewalks with steps. The street looks unpaved, but is firmly packed by traffic. The license plate on the car is L2999. The model is unknown, but the date of the picture is 1936. (Courtesy of the Pittsburgh City Photographer Collection, Archives Service Center, University of Pittsburgh.)

This picture was taken in 1931 to show the condition of the streets and the neighborhood for a study. A man sits on his porch on Manor Street. The automobile parked on the street has no tires. The houses were eventually razed. (Courtesy of the Pittsburgh City Photographer Collection, Archives Service Center, University of Pittsburgh.)

One wonders if horses and mules traversed Vinecliff Street. Today, a steep set of steps provide access from Wyoming Street all the way down to East Sycamore Street. The old right-of-way is clearly discernable although much too vertical for today's vehicles. Many of the homes are abandoned, a testament to the difficulty of moving furniture and appliances along the steps. Pictured are the houses on one side of the steps only, while houses further down change to the other side of the steps. Nowhere on Vinecliff Street do houses face each other. (Courtesy of Michael J. Liss.)

These houses are near the bottom of Vinecliff Street, closer to Sycamore Street. The house in the middle of the photograph is stately, reminiscent of a large farmhouse. Only the porch can be seen of the house on the right, which is partially demolished. The steps egress into a short "street" which is about 30 feet from East Sycamore Street. This street leads to a site where an old home for unwed mothers was once located. This home was demolished to make room for the P. J. McArdle Roadway Bridge. (Courtesy of Michael J. Liss.)

This large house at 413 Bailey Avenue was built in 1883 according to its cornerstone. It was owned by the Robinson Family and later was bought by a Bailey family who may or may not have been one of the original Baileys. It was extensively remodeled in 1989, but the letter "R," etched in the glass entry door, was left intact. Mr. Robinson had been a steamboat captain.

The Martin family lived in this home at 736 Wills Street. George and Marie Martin had six children, all of whom walked 10 minutes each way to St. Justin Elementary School. It is a large house, large enough to accommodate its eight residents. The family eventually moved to Mount Lebanon, but the children rode the streetcar to St. Justin High School and still had to walk up Lelia Street to get there. (Courtesy of Janet Martin Fagan.)

Commonly called "the Junction" because so many routes meet there, it is at the base of Lelia Street, reached by the steps on the left. Houses were built on the crests of both hills. Streetcars going through the tunnel under Mount Washington and then crossing the Smithfield Street Bridge over the Monongahela River finally arrive in downtown Pittsburgh. (Courtesy of Pennsylvania Department, Pittsburgh Photographic Library, Carnegie Library of Pittsburgh.)

Ladies disembark from a No. 46 Carrick streetcar at the South Hills Junction and either transfer to another streetcar or walk up Lelia Street to their homes. The year is 1916, and the streetcar tunnel, built in 1904, provided easy access to the city for the people of the South Hills. The Railway Tunnels were cut through almost solid rock at a cost of $835,000. The first route number to Mount Washington was car No. 213. (Courtesy of the Pittsburgh City Photographer Collection, Archives Service Center, University of Pittsburgh.)

This photograph shows a family standing on the porch of a beautiful old home in January 1926. The family is not identified, but the house on Mount Washington Roadway is typical of the homes in that area of Mount Washington. The P. J. McArdle Roadway was to be constructed and paved in 1928, so it is likely that this house was either destroyed or moved to another location. (Courtesy of the Pittsburgh City Photographer Collection, Archives Service Center, University of Pittsburgh.)

This July 31, 1937, photograph shows the intersection of Mount Washington Roadway and Grandview Avenue. The roadway had already been named to honor P. J. McArdle, and Grandview Avenue still had streetcar tracks. The traffic divider is no longer there. The Gulf Building is in the background. The house on the right has been made into apartments. A store in the distance is Rosenbaum's, now long gone. (Courtesy of the Pittsburgh City Photographer Collection, Archives Service Center, University of Pittsburgh.)

This picture was taken on June 8, 1931, to determine the condition of a road. If the Mount Washington Roadway Extension were to be built, this lovely old house would also be in danger of being demolished to make way for the extension. (Courtesy of the Pittsburgh City Photographer Collection, Archives Service Center, University of Pittsburgh.)

The Monongahela Incline was opened May 28, 1870. Eventually, Pittsburgh had 17 inclines. Now only two remain. The Mon Incline was first operated by the Pittsburgh Railways Company, and in 1964, it was taken over by the Port Authority. A half-million people, including commuters and visitors, ride this incline each year. This incline climbs a 35 percent grade, which is one of the steepest incline grades in the world. In 1970, the History and Landmarks Foundation declared it an historic structure. (Courtesy of Library and Archives Division, Historical Society of Western Pennsylvania, Pittsburgh.)

Pictured in this June 1933 photograph is one part of the Shiloh business district with the Freyvogel Pharmacy to the right. A dentist, Dr. Villanova has his office on the second floor. Next door is the South Hills Trust Company at 124 Shiloh Street. Down the street, Bard's advertises ice cream. (Courtesy of the Pittsburgh City Photographer Collection, Archives Service Center, University of Pittsburgh.)

On April 30, 1934, Boggs Avenue looked like this. Supermarkets had arrived. Kroger's was on the left and several cars were parked on the street, presumably to shop. What a marvel it was to have a store that supplied all kinds of groceries, meats, and sundries all in one place. The A&P had already entered the market, and people traveled from far and wide to try it out. Some people had to borrow a car to get to the store, since not everyone owned his own. Dick H. Thomas Drugs and other stores were on the left. (Courtesy of the Pittsburgh City Photographer Collection, Archives Service Center, University of Pittsburgh.)

The rebuilding of Mount Washington Roadway was underway on August 12, 1927. The cobblestones in the front were removed to make way for another surface. Note the steps to the house at the top of the picture. (Courtesy of the Pittsburgh City Photographer Collection, Archives Service Center, University of Pittsburgh.)

J. G. Wild built this lovely old building in 1903. He is pictured here in the middle of two men with a customer on the left and his grandson on the right. It was the Christmas holiday. There is a star in the window and a bell on the telegraph pole. Notice the rack of straw brooms in front of the store and the barbershop pole hanging next-door. Wild's family lived on the second floor. When he retired, an unidentified person opened a bakery in the store. This bakery remained there until 1931 when Herman Knell Sr. opened his bakery and called it Knell's. His daughter-in-law Lois Wild Knell was the granddaughter of J. G. Wild. (Courtesy of Lois Knell.)

In this 1941 photograph, the salesgirls of Knell's bakery celebrate its 10th anniversary. Located at the corner of Virginia Avenue and Shiloh Street, the building has housed three generations of Wild family businesses. Begun by J. G. Wild as a grocery store in 1903, it was later owned by Wild's granddaughter Lois Knell. Her husband, Herman or "Herky," bought the store and became one of the best bakers in the area. (Courtesy of Lois Knell.)

Notice that this gas station had 10 gasoline pumps. Owned by Paul Wild, the station sold two grades of gasoline for five different oil companies. That would be unthinkable today. The companies were Amoco, Sunoco, Texaco, Esso, and Atlantic. On the site today is a BP station. Wild's Lubrication building was built on the steep Wyoming Street, fronting on Virginia Avenue. Next door is the fire station. (Courtesy of Lois Knell.)

Pictured in 1990 is the Wick Lumber Company at 309 Bailey Avenue. Originally on Judicial Street with a stable at the rear of the building, it specialized in prefabricated houses. They built many of the homes in the old Bailey farm, which comprised most of the land between Bailey Avenue and Warrington Avenue, and between Beltzhoover Avenue and Ruth Street. Due to neighbors' complaints about a possible fire hazard, the company moved to 1916 Bigby Street. (Courtesy of Michael J. Liss.)

Robert Wick is pictured in the office of Wick Lumber. Wick was the third generation proprietor of his company. After complaints by neighbors, he moved his company to Bigby Street, but again, due to pressure from the city to make his land a playground, Wick moved again to Bailey Avenue. After his death, the property was sold and the lumberyard was demolished in 2006. The land is now a playground. (Courtesy of Michael J. Liss.)

A page filled with advertisements for area stores appeared in the *Mount Washington and Duquesne Heights News* in 1907. The page was reprinted in the centennial edition of the *Mount Washington News*.

35

Knell's bakery, like so many other Mount Washington family businesses, remained in the family for years. Herky Knell Jr. learned the business from his father and did much of the baking. Frank Briganti of Chess Street remembers his mother asking him to walk several blocks every Saturday to get the family's treats for the weekend. In 1954, a loaf of bread cost 20¢, and layer cakes were 49¢. A family could buy both for 69¢. Knell's products were so popular that they sold in many other areas of the city, and their wedding cakes were so good that they were carried as far away as Chicago and New York. (Courtesy of Lois Knell.)

Herky Knell (right) obviously enjoys his own bakery products. Pictured with his son, Keith (center), and Al Mazzarini (left) enjoying a crème puff, his bakery was a must-stop for residents of the hill. Herky was not only a wonderful baker but also a talented organist. He and his wife, Lois, both played organ for the Grandview United Presbyterian Church in Mount Washington and for the Baptist Church in Mount Lebanon. (Courtesy of Lois Knell.)

While his family lived next door in a small house, John Dierker built this larger house in 1927. He ran the store as a grocery for an unknown number of years. John and Virginia Peden purchased it in 1958 from the heirs of John Dierker. It was typical of the corner grocery of the period but became outdated when the supermarkets came into existence. Virginia closed the store in 1980 after her husband died. She later sold it to a young man and his father. The street next to it is West Sycamore Street. The railing is to aid walkers down the concrete steps that once were a boardwalk. The street is paved now but probably was not in 1927 when the store was built. (Courtesy of Virginia Peden.)

Standing in front of his store at 610 Southern Avenue is Frank Stang. His daughter, Bernice, sits at his feet. Opened in 1917, Stang's Grocery served the people of the area for over 60 years. The owner worked 60 hours a week, as did his son Francis, or "Bud." Though initially a meat market, in 1930, Frank expanded and sold groceries. For 20 years the Stang's lived on a 12-acre farm in Peter's Township, commuting daily to and from the store. "In those days," Frank said, "the commute took only 20 minutes since there were no stoplights until you hit Mount Lebanon." His granddaughter Mary Deschler remembers helping out at the store, and delivering orders. Frank Stang died in 1979 at his home behind the store. He worked every day until his death. (Courtesy of Mary Deschler.)

Guy Galasso and Elva Collyer pose in their newly painted building, which houses Collyer Realty on Boggs Avenue. Galasso worked for the company and studied to become a broker. When the Collyer family gave up the business, he took over and retained the name. He was a 1944 graduate of St. Justin High School and was instrumental in organizing and gathering graduates for class reunions. (Courtesy of William Galasso.)

James Bensor Lash founded Lash Realty in 1880. He began with an office at 317 Virginia Avenue, but soon moved to 530 Grandview Avenue where he made a section of his large home into an office. Pictured here are, from left to right, Al Schmidt, Ed Voigt, Sadie Maust Lash, and James Bensor Lash. Maust and Elva Collyer (pictured above) were friendly competitors as the only two women realtors in the area. (Courtesy of William Goodboy.)

Three

BEAUTIFICATION OF THE HILL

In 1945, Gilbert Love wrote in his daily column, "Has it ever occurred to you about this time of year what a beautiful sight it would be if the steep Mount Washington hillside were covered with some sort of flowering tree, shrub, or vines?" The Mount Washington and Duquesne Heights hillside has been the subject of discussion between the city of Pittsburgh and Mount Washington for almost 100 years. In 1912, J. E. Richie proposed that the bluff be covered with apartment buildings. The Gossar Plan came later, calling for a two-level bridge, starting at Shingess Street and Forbes Avenue with a tunnel under Mount Washington emerging at Haberman Street and Warrington Avenue. In 1915, area women planted shrubs and flowers on the hill. In 1928, the City of Pittsburgh's Planning Commission approved a $75,000 planting program. The Depression caused the plan to be abandoned. In 1953, the Mount Washington Hillside Planting Committee was formed under the chairmanship of Verna Dibble. Some of the committee's goals were to not allow billboards, commercial development, or obstruction of the view. One of their first missions was the removal of billboards from the hillside. On March 18, 1955, the Pittsburgh Brewing Company announced that they would cancel the lease for the giant beer sign on the hillside. In addition, they gave $100 to the planting committee. Annual Arbor Day celebrations were held on Grandview Avenue from 1953 until 1963. Trees were planted every year. Both mayors David Lawrence and Joseph M. Barr participated in the tree planting ceremonies throughout the years.

And now, in 2006, the Heinz Endowments has approved $150,000 toward the development of the Grandview Scenic Byways Park on Mount Washington. The Pittsburgh City Council voted to create the park in Mount Washington and Duquesne Heights, consisting of 250 acres of city-owned land that nearly encircles the two neighborhoods. It includes existing parks and hillsides. On October 25, 2006, a statue of Guyasuta, a Seneca leader, and George Washington, sculpted by James West, was dedicated. Called *Point of View*, the statue is located near Sweetbriar Street in Duquesne Heights.

In the early part of the 20th century, the hill soaring up over 500 feet to Mount Washington was dirty, dingy, dangerous, and weed strewn, having huge pock marks caused by coal mining and neglect. Around 1915, clubwomen from the city of Pittsburgh decided to brave the restrictions of such height and plant flowers in an effort to beautify the mount. They were among the first in a long stream of women hoping to achieve that same goal. (Courtesy of Pennsylvania Department, Pittsburgh Photographic Library, Carnegie Library.)

In 1932, this beautiful Victorian home was torn down by the City of Pittsburgh, permitted under eminent domain regulations, to provide for the widening of P. J. McArdle Roadway. Located on Grandview Avenue, the owner, Margaret Gavin, hoped to receive $11,000, but the city paid only $7,500. (Courtesy of William Goodboy.)

With St. Mary of the Mount Catholic Church in the background, Mayor Joseph Barr and Verna Dibble observe students from South Hills High School pet a dog as they rest from planting a tree on the hillside. Every year, students from local schools competed to win the honor of planting a tree on Arbor Day. (Courtesy of Lani F. Fritz.)

Observing the annual Arbor Day on April 10, 1956, is a crowd of residents. With the city of Pittsburgh in the background, Mayor David Lawrence presides over the ceremony to dedicate the planting of a scarlet oak tree on the hillside. The South Hills High School band provided entertainment. (Courtesy of Lani F. Fritz.)

41

In 1963, an annual Arbor Day celebration was held on Grandview Avenue. The overlooks were not yet built, so a platform was built for Robert J. Templeton, director of the department of parks and recreation, to offer remarks. (Courtesy of Lani F. Fritz.)

The band director from South Hills High School conducts the band as it performs on Grandview Avenue in 1963. It is reported that this was the last Arbor Day celebration. Verna Dibble, who spearheaded the planting committee and its Arbor Day celebrations, had died. (Courtesy of Angela C. Kennedy.)

Seen from the top of the Liberty Tubes, the Panhandle Division Bridge is to the left of the Liberty Bridge. Built in 1928 by Allegheny County, the Liberty Bridge is 2,663 feet long. The decorative traffic circle, built at the intersection of the bridge and the Mount Washington Roadway, was eventually eliminated. In the distance is the Gulf Building and next to it is the beacon that spells Pittsburgh in Morse code. (Courtesy of the University of Pittsburgh.)

The Smithfield Street Bridge was paved on June 6, 1922. Five types of conveyances are evident in this photograph: the incline tracks to the right usually have a car (though not visible in this photograph), the automobile, the taxicab leaving the station, the streetcar, and the horse and wagon. Advertisements cover the hill. It was signs such as these that Verna Dibble and her women's group protested, although the beer sign was the worst offender according to the group. (Courtesy of the Pittsburgh City Photographer Collection, Archives Service Center, University of Pittsburgh.)

This photograph shows Bigham House on the grounds of Chatham Village at 655 Pennridge Road. Built in 1844, this red brick Greek Revival style house is now called Chatham Hall. It was once the home of Thomas J. and Maria L. Bigham. Known as the sage of Mount Washington, he was an attorney, newspaper publisher, politician, and abolitionist. Old family histories note that this house was used as a stop on the Underground Railroad. (Courtesy of Michael J. Liss.)

Chatham Village is a planned community from the 1930s built by the Buhl Foundation as a for-profit investment and as a national example of high quality middle class housing. An innovative layout by America's preeminent garden city planners, Clarence Stein and Henry Wright, put curved streets at the perimeter of nearly 200 attractive red brick Colonial Revival style row houses on landscaped garden courtyards and hillside terraces. The neighborhood became a cooperative in 1960 and is a national historic landmark. It is part of the hill, and has added to the beautification of Duquesne Heights. (Courtesy of David Vater.)

Four

THE PEOPLE WHO
LIVE HERE

Pittsburgh's setting is the gift of nature. However, its development depends on the people who made it their own, lived in it, and took care of it. Its industry, architecture, and livability are the results of the industriousness and deep affection the people of Pittsburgh have for their city. This affection includes the whole of the city; its industry, its sports teams, their neighbors; their neighborliness and openness to newcomers. As two neighborhoods of Pittsburgh, Mount Washington and Duquesne Heights have some desirable, unique characteristics of their own. As Leonard Skirboll exclaimed, "People from Mount Washington, stay in Mount Washington." Historically it seems true, as evidenced by the names of the people, the inter-marriages of the early settlers, and the names of the streets, reflecting early families. Bigham Street was initially Maria Street and changed to Bigham after Maria's marriage to Thomas Bigham. Boggs was named after the Boggs family. Kirkpatrick Road was named for Maj. Abraham Kirkpatrick, an early landowner. McArdle Roadway was named for Peter J. McArdle, a city councilman. Soffel Street was named for Jacob Soffel and Judge Sara Soffel, and Minsinger Street was named for Jacob Minsinger, a businessman. Most of the names of streets were changed when the City of Pittsburgh annexed Mount Washington and Duquesne Heights to the city in 1872. An example of a community on the top of Sycamore Street is Little Italy. As told by Virginia Peden, Little Italy consisted of 30 wooden houses with no electricity and no paved streets, yet the residents enjoyed life with all its struggles and hardships.

The Kimmerle family was gathered to celebrate the birthday of one of the grandchildren. Joseph Kimmerle, standing on the left, lived on Sycamore Street with his wife Mary, shown with her hand on her hip. Together they raised seven children; three were born at 210 Southern Avenue and four at 2 Sycamore Street. Four of their daughters are pictured here: Genevieve, first row beside the little boy; Mamie, with the baby; Hilda, to the right of her mother; and Ethel, second from the right. Sitting in the back with the dark dress is Walburga Kirchensteiner Kimmerle, the great-grandmother of the baby. She lived to be 92 years old.

Mary Adley Kimmerle was a young woman whose parents came from Ireland. She was born in downtown Pittsburgh in 1872 when it was common for people to live in the city. She told her grandchildren that she was raised on Strawberry Way in downtown Pittsburgh. After her marriage, she lived at 210 Southern Avenue where three of her seven children were born.

From left to right, sisters Hazel, Ruth, and Marie Hall from Mount Washington recline in the backyard of their home on Grandview Avenue with an unidentified friend, and their mother Bridget Madden Hall watching in the background. This photograph was taken during the Depression when families often moved from home to home. Later, the Hall family finally moved into their permanent home on Merrimac Street. (Courtesy of Jerome Hall Schwertz.)

Posing on a wooden boardwalk in their backyard on Grandview Avenue are the Hall sisters. The girls lived there with their parents at a time when there were no outlooks or tourist attractions. They lived a quiet life, attending school and church at St. Mary of the Mount within walking distance of their home. Hazel is also pictured in the graduating class of 1915 from St. Mary of the Mount High School, seen on the bottom of page 79. (Courtesy of Jerome Hall Schwertz.)

This natty couple—she in knickers and he with his straw hat—sit on the bumper of his car. Jerome and Marie Hall Schwertz lived on several streets in Mount Washington: Amabel Street, Hallock Street, and finally Merrimac Street. They were married in St. Mary of the Mount Catholic Church in 1927. (Courtesy of Jerome Hall Schwertz.)

Francis and Bea Schroth are showns all dressed up on their wedding day. (Courtesy of Jerome Hall Schwertz.)

In 1923, these children attended a cat party at Ream Playground. The girls wore dresses and they wore bags on their heads with eyes cut out. There were no cats in sight, only one dog. Ream Park was and still is a good spot for children's and adult's activities. (Courtesy of the Pittsburgh City Photographer Collection, Archives Service Center, University of Pittsburgh.)

It is not known why all these children were gathered together on June 8, 1931. They formed a pyramid and those at the top were holding on for dear life. The two houses and car were located on Excelsior Street, looking from Manor Street east to the Schoeber and Patacki property. (Courtesy of the Pittsburgh City Photographer Collection, Archives Service Center, University of Pittsburgh.)

Mark, Joe, Bill, and Fred Smallhoover lived at 220 Merrimac Street. Their parents, Joseph and Evelyn, moved to Mount Washington from Allentown in the early 1920s. Merrimac Street was paved with cobblestones. Mark remembers that while the stones were being laid, the boys helped themselves to some of the blocks and built a wall in their backyard. Four of the boys attended St. Mary of the Mount Elementary School and High School, while Jack went to St. Vincent Preparatory School. Mark recalled that three doors down from them, the cellar of the house caved in because of a mine shaft. This worried his parents until they found that the mine shaft was in their backyard and not under their house. (Courtesy of Mark Smallhoover.)

In this photograph, Anton Kushbaugh, Mark Smallhoover, Francis Malloy, Eddie Boylan, and James Curley sit together. It was 1941 and the boys' graduation from St. Mary of the Mount High School was just around the corner. But, unbeknownst to them, December was to bring the bombing of Pearl Harbor and a change in all of their lives. Smallhoover went into the U.S. Navy, and Kushbaugh became a pilot. The others served in the army. (Courtesy of Mark Smallhoover.)

This photograph from the winter of 1938 shows, from left to right, cousins Janet Martin and Eileen Burge playing in the snow with neighbor Nancy Lee in the backyard of 736 Wills Street where the Martin family lived. (Courtesy of Janet Martin Fagan.)

The Toonerville Trolley, as it was playfully called, is going down Woodruff Street on tracks laid out practically in the front yard of the Lash home at 371 Woodruff Street. Standing in the front yard are, from left to right, (first row) Melvin LeBaron; (second row) Grace Lash and Alice Getty; (third row) Mabel Maust. As an adult, Grace Lash joined Lash Realty in 1971 when her mother, Sadie Lash, died. She remained in business until she retired on December 1, 1990. She was well known and was loved by many Mount Washington residents. Among her many friends were the Minsingers and the Soffels. (Courtesy of William Goodboy.)

This healthy, pretty, young woman, Ethel Kimmerle, lived on Sycamore Street in a house built by her grandfather, Wilhelm Kimmerle. Wilhelm, a carpenter in his native Germany, immigrated to America after serving in the 1870–1871 Victories War, where he was awarded a Bronze Medal by the Kaiser. Ethel, born in 1899, shared the house with her parents, Joseph and Mary, her two brothers, Bill and Joe, and her four sisters, Mamie, Gen, Hilda, and Mildred. She married, had no children, and died from tuberculosis in Arizona where her father had sent her, hoping for a cure.

Joseph Kimmerle married Mary Emma Adley on August 1, 1893. They raised seven children in Mount Washington, before moving to Beechview in 1916. Although Joseph's father Wilhelm had built the home on Sycamore Street, Joseph thought that the house did not have enough room or conveniences. They had to get water from a spring at the side of the house. It was ice cold and the family kept butter and root beer on shelves built into the wall. There was no cellar and the outhouse was in the backyard.

Does anyone like oranges? In 1910, the writer of the above invitation thought so. She asked that each of the children she invited bring a dozen of them. The writer was Hilda Kimmerle and the hill was Sycamore Street, known then as the Burma Road. The part of Sycamore where they lived is closed now to accommodate Pittsburgh's Light Rail System trolley stop.

Sycamore Street is halfway up the front slope of Mount Washington. Its residents looked down on the Monongahela River and the bridge to the Golden Triangle, although it was not called that in the early 1900s when this picture was drawn. Genevieve Kimmerle, who lived at two Sycamore Street from her birth until 1910, drew the kitchen from memory in the 1930s. Notice the wood or coal burning chimney on the stove, and the hurricane lantern on the table. This kitchen provided sustenance and family life for the family of Joseph Kimmerle.

Mary Louise Paff was born and raised on Southern Avenue, the only child of George and Lila Rice Paff. Notice the little boots and the long stockings. This was the style of the period, about 1920. Paff's parents called her "Pet," which was appropriate for an only, beloved child. Considered a talented pianist and a child prodigy, she had a radio program on KDKA radio. After attending Mount Mercy College she married George Doschek, a violinist. They both played with the Pittsburgh Symphony Orchestra. In addition, she also performed at New York's Town Hall.

George Otto Paff, sitting, poses with two of his colleagues. He and his wife, Lila, lived on Southern Avenue, where they raised one child, Mary Louise. George was a traveling salesman for the Richardson Company.

George Boxheimer was a clerk for the Pittsburgh City Council. It was he who was instrumental in flooding Olympia Park in the winter to create an ice skating rink for the neighborhood. Many residents remember how much fun it was, especially the big bonfire that warmed the skaters. Pictured at a concert at Olympia Park in the summer is George, his wife, Julia, and their child, Francis, who later died in the flu epidemic of 1918. (Courtesy of Mary Boxheimer.)

In the early days of the 20th century, families did not have play gyms. Instead, they built their own swings by swinging a rope around a strong branch of a tree and placing a sanded board between the ropes to form a seat. Julia Boxheimer enjoys her swing on a nice summer day on Olympia Street. (Courtesy of Mary Boxheimer.)

This interesting home was listed for rent by Sadie Lash of Lash Realty for an annual fee of $630. It had five rooms on the first floor and a second floor apartment for adults only. Washbasins were supplied in every bedroom; it had built-in equipment, hot water, and hot air heat. Because the writing on the back of the picture was not clear, the $630 fee may have been only for the apartment. It is hard to believe that a whole house could be rented for that amount! (Courtesy of William Goodboy.)

In 1914, this grocery was located at 51 Shiloh Street and was owned by James A. Whitehead who lived on Joel's Lane (now Amabel Street). He was selling Campbell's soup, cans of corn, vegetables, or pears at a price of three for 25¢. Oddly, he also sold oysters and had a pantry and games available. Pictured here are, from left to right, Samuel Lewis, delivery boy; William Francis Burns, clerk and grandfather of William Goodboy; Thomas Whitehead, clerk; and the owner, James A. Whitehead. (Courtesy of William Goodboy.)

Julia and George Boxheimer pose with their son, Francis. Even though it was a picnic, George wore his vest and tie. Young Francis is wearing a tunic-type white suit. (Courtesy of Mary Boxheimer.)

Marie Hall celebrates her first communion at St. Mary of the Mount Catholic Church in the early 1900s. First communions are special and a new dress and new shoes are required, not by the church, but by excited students. Hall probably wore the dress only a few times for weekly mass, until it was passed on to another girl in the next first communion class. The Halls lived on Amabel Street. (Courtesy of Jerome Hall Schwertz.)

Posing here is a group of people having a picnic. Bridget Madden Hall, the mother of Hazel, Ruth, and Marie Hall, is in the third row. Her daughters are in the first row on the right, beside the boys. Everyone is dressed for a celebration, but maybe that was the custom in the early 1900s for a picnic. The gentleman in the top row with the pencil mark above his head is Mr. Madden. (Courtesy of Jerome Hall Schwertz.)

Residence 114 Boggs Avenue, Mt. Washington, Pittsburgh, Pa.

A family poses in front of their home at 114 Boggs Avenue. What a surprise it was to William Galasso when a friend showed him this postcard. It was his home, although the number was different. And here it was on a postcard sent by an unknown person and found by a friend. When Galasso was only seven years old, his father, Benjamin, purchased the house. He believes that the woman and children pictured are the Robinson's, the previous owners of the house at 428 Boggs Avenue. (Courtesy of William Galasso.)

Benjamin Galasso poses in front of his home at 428 Boggs Avenue. Galasso came to the United States in 1920. After living for some years on Albert Street, he bought the house on Boggs Street. The home is now 110 years old. A real estate dealer, he sold homes in the hill district of Pittsburgh, traveling always on foot and by trolley. He never owned a car. Galasso was an expert drummer and flute player. (Courtesy of William Galasso.)

Returning in 1986 to check out the old homestead is Frank Briganti who lived at 605 Chess Street from 1932 until 1947, when he graduated from St. Justin High School. After graduating, he enrolled at Georgetown University. He now lives in Austin, Texas. (Courtesy of Frank Briganti.)

Pictured is Christina Zink Soffel. Not the Mrs. Soffel of movie fame, but the mother of Peter Soffel, the warden of the Allegheny County Jail. Katherine Soffel, the warden's wife, was the subject of an MGM movie, *Mrs. Soffel*. She helped two men who had been convicted of murder escape from the Allegheny County Jail. Commonly referred to as the Biddle Boys, the brothers, Ed and Jack, were captured along with Katherine and all were shot. The Biddle boys died, but Katherine survived and spent 20 months in jail. It was reported that she never again saw her four children. She became a seamstress to support herself, and five years later in 1909, she died from typhoid fever at age 42. (Courtesy of Mary Soffel.)

The Soffel family played a large role in public affairs in Mount Washington and in Pittsburgh. Pictured is Carrie Elizabeth and her husband Walter Soffel, the younger brother of Peter, the warden. Their son Gordon's wife, Mary Soffel, has kept scrapbooks and pictures about her husband's family. Easily remembered would be Sara M. Soffel, the first woman judge of a criminal court in Pennsylvania. The elder Peter Soffel came to Mount Washington in 1859, and lived where Julius Wild's store later stood. When Mount Washington was still a borough, he served two terms as a councilman. Jacob Soffel, another brother of Peter Sr., served as an alderman. A street was named after the Soffels to honor their contributions to Mount Washington. (Courtesy of Mary Soffel.)

What a splendid home. Located at 530 Grandview Avenue, it was the home of James Bensor Lash, an early realtor in Mount Washington. Standing on the porch are (left to right) Lash, his housekeeper Ella Davies, and Ida Belle Lent Lash, his wife. James remodeled the left section of his home to create an office for his company, Lash Realty. Unfortunately, in 1932, this home and its neighbor were demolished in order to widen P. J. McArdle Roadway. The office was then moved to its final location at 120 Shiloh Street. (Courtesy of William Goodboy.)

The family of James Bensor Lash is pictured here. From left to right are (first row) Lash and his wife, Ida Belle Lent Lash; (second row) Clarence Ellwood Lash, Ethel Leona Lash Burns, James Harvey Lash, and Frank Horace Lash. J. Harvey Lash was the father of Grace Lash. It was he who took over the Lash Realty when his father died in 1917, and when he died in 1923, his wife, Sadie Maust Lash, Grace's mother, took the reins. It was Grace who ran the business until 1990. By then, the firm had been in business for over 100 years. (Courtesy of William Goodboy.)

This picture was discovered in the archives of the Mount Washington Library, but it had no documentation. It is assumed that the men pictured here on July 1918, were going to war, for on April 6, 1917, the United States had declared war on Germany. The 100 day offensive (the last 100 days of World War I) began on August 8, 1918. Armistice Day was celebrated on November 11, but is now called Veterans Day to honor the veterans of all recent wars. (Courtesy of Carnegie Library, Mount Washington branch.)

The Castle Shannon Incline carried both freight and passengers. Robert Wick, the owner of Wick lumber, remembers hauling lumber via horse-drawn wagons from a boxcar at the Old Pittsburgh and Lake Erie Railroad, now known as Station Square. The Castle Shannon Incline made this possible. It was the third incline built by the Pittsburgh and Castle Shannon Railroad. The original was built to haul coal from the saddle area of Mount Washington to Carson Street. (Courtesy of Pittsburgh Railways Company, Archives Service Center, University of Pittsburgh.)

Five

FAITH

The establishment of churches of many denominations evidences that faith was an important component in the development of Mount Washington and Duquesne Heights. As soon as people began to live and work there, and as they began to congregate there, they began to pray there. There were only two churches in Pittsburgh in 1790. A mission Sunday school was conducted on Coal Hill as early as 1833. The Mount Washington Presbyterian Church was organized on June 20, 1857. As more people decided to live on the hill, more denominations built places of worship. Grace Episcopal Church was organized in 1852; the Methodist Church in 1866; the Baptist Church in 1866; the German Evangelical in 1873; the United Presbyterian in 1883; the Lutheran Church in 1883; the Methodist Protestant in 1890; the Nazarene Church in 1898; St. Mary of the Mount Catholic Church in 1873; and St. Justin Catholic Church in 1917. These churches and others who have organized since still serve the residents of the area. Also, begun in 2004, the Urban Mountain Gathering Place plays a role in providing activities to members of the church, the school, and the community. Non-denominational, it has been instrumental in the progress of Grandview Elementary School by supporting the after-school tutoring program. The Urban Mountain Gathering Place also has been helpful working with the Grand View Scenic Byways Park by planning the design, lobbying government officials, and holding meetings in the Presbyterian church on Bailey Avenue.

In this photograph, St. Mary of the Mount Catholic Church celebrates its 100th anniversary with a special mass in 1969. The main celebrants were Bishop Vincent Leonard and the pastor, Msgr. Joseph Knorr. St. Mary's was established in 1869 as a mission of St. Malachy's on the South Side. With the building of the inclines in 1869 and 1877, the population of Coal Hill increased so much that there was the need for a larger church. The present church was dedicated on December 19, 1897. The building cost $115,000 to build. (Courtesy of St. Mary of the Mount Alumni Association.)

Sister Herberta taught school at St. Mary of the Mount High School. She was the homeroom teacher of the freshman class and taught Latin and English. She was a well-loved lady according to one of her students who later became a nun herself. She is pictured here outside of the high school. (Courtesy of St. Mary of the Mount Alumni Association.)

St. Justin Catholic Church, located on Lelia Street, has served the people of Mount Washington since 1917. Known originally known as St. Justin the Martyr, the name was simplified to St. Justin. Originally, masses were held in the Lincoln Theater at 121 Boggs Avenue. Land was bought in the present location in 1921 and a church was built in 1923. The parish had an elementary school and a high school, both of which are now closed.

Seen on the bottom of page 79, Gerald Schroth was pictured in the St. Mary of the Mount High School graduation class of 1915. Ten years later, shown here, is the card from the celebration of his first mass after his ordination to the priesthood on June 20, 1925. (Courtesy of Jerome Hall Schwertz.)

This large group of boys and girls are celebrating May Day on the lawn of St. Justin Catholic Church side yard in 1921. May Day was a pleasant celebration for the children. They got to pick one of their own to be the May Day queen, and could dress up in their fine clothes, some even wearing their first communion outfits. All could wear flower garlands on their heads, and some could carry bouquets. The picture was taken from Lelia and Boggs Avenues looking north toward Paul Street. The house behind the children was used as the rectory, and later as the

convent. The present church now sits on this site. Formerly, the house and land belonged to Maria Boggs Foster, daughter of David Boggs. Paul Street was named after John Paul, a friend of the Boggs family and a haberdasher in downtown Pittsburgh. He also owned land in the Boggs Avenue area. The convent of St. Justin, which housed the Sisters of Mercy, was later located on Boggs Avenue. It was designed by architects Kaiser, Neal, and Reid and was built in 1939. The chapel of St. Justin's was designed by Carlton Strong and built in 1918.

Bishop John Deardon officiates at the blessing of St. Mary of the Mount High School on December 16, 1956. He later became archbishop of Detroit in 1958 and was created cardinal in 1969 by Pope Pius XIII. (Courtesy of St. Mary of the Mount Alumni Association.)

Pictured in 1966 at a luncheon meeting are the Sisters of the Immaculate Heart of Mary. Sister Geraldine is sitting on the right, fourth from the end, with Sister Feldecamp to her right. Sister Thomasita is on the left, third from the end. The other nuns are not identified. The sisters of the Immaculate Heart of Mary were the first and only order of nuns to teach at St. Mary of the Mount High School. (Courtesy of St. Mary of the Mount Alumni Association.)

Boys in Catholic schools could be altar boys or choirboys if they chose. Their tasks were different and their attire differed but their dedication was exemplary. Choirboys had a desire to sing, and many had glorious voices, at least until they reached adolescence. They wore large bows at their necks to distinguish them from the altar boys. Altar boys chose to serve on the altar with the priest. The mischievous looks on some of the altar boys faces may indicate that they enjoyed not having the large bows at their necks. These boys were photographed in 1956. (Courtesy of St. Mary of the Mount Alumni Association.)

The Zion Evangelical Lutheran Church sits at the corner of Smith Way and Boggs Avenue. It is the former site of the home and estate of John Paul who married Elizabeth, the widow of William Boggs.

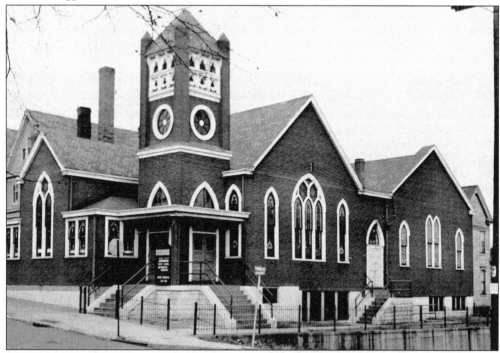

The Haven Methodist (Episcopal) Church and the Washington Heights Methodist (Protestant) Church consolidated in 1954 to become Haven Heights United Methodist Church. Both churches have served the people of Mount Washington since the late 1880s. (Courtesy of Cel Mazzarini.)

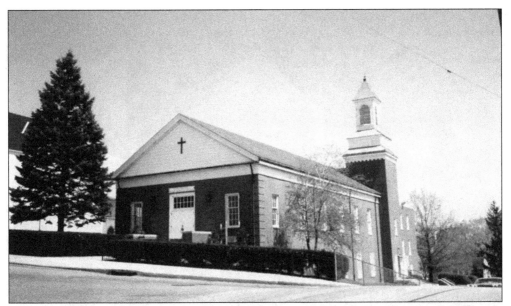

Pictured in 1989 is the third church building housing the Haven Heights United Methodist Church after two others had been destroyed by fire. There have been many other destructive fires over the years, and the *Mount Washington News* reported that churches have been the suffered a great deal, among them the Mount Washington Methodist, Washington Heights Methodist in 1898, Grace Episcopal in 1923, and the First German E. P. Church in 1914. (Courtesy of Cel Mazzarini.)

Who are these dressed up children? Are they waiting for a showboat? That could be, because they are dressed to perform in the musical *Showboat* with the adult choir in 1963. Both groups sang with the Grandview United Presbyterian Church. The proceeds from the musical were contributed to the fund to purchase a much-needed organ. (Courtesy of Lois Knell.)

The adult choir of the Grandview United Presbyterian Church performed the musical *Showboat* together with the children's choir. A much larger group than the children's choir, but together they succeeded in raising money toward the purchase of a new organ. (Courtesy of Lois Knell.)

Ruth F. Hall lived at 607 Grandview Avenue when this picture was taken in the late 1920s. She was prepared for a service at church, possibly confirmation. (Courtesy of Jerome Hall Schwertz.)

Six

THE EDUCATION OF
OUR CHILDREN

The strength of any community is its children. People were living in Mount Washington and Duquesne Heights very early in the 19th century. The earliest public school was established in Pittsburgh in 1835, although there were some private schools. Before that, children were sent east to school if the parents could afford it. Little learning was necessary for the life they would live on the farm, in the mines, or in the glass factories. There were approximately 10,000 boys under the age of 16 working in the glass factories. The U.S. Census of 1900 reported that 675,342 boys and 391,982 girls between the ages of 10 and 14 were employed in factories, mines, and sweatshops in the United States. It is not recorded how many children from the mount were employed in the mines and factories, but considering the hardships of making a living in the 18th century, it is a surety that the percentage was high. For more than 100 years the manufacture of glass was centered in Pittsburgh. It was possible because of the availability of coal from Coal Hill. The glasshouse boys played a central role in the industry that helped make Pittsburgh an industrial giant. Formal education for many had to wait.

However, not everyone waited. As more and more people reached the land above the river, churches were built, businesses opened, and schools were built. Cargo School was established in 1896. It was reported in the *Mount Washington and Duquesne Heights Newspaper* of 1907 that the ninth annual commencement of Mount Washington schools was held in the Pentacostal church. Prospect School opened in 1871. It was regarded as a monument to the success of Robert Moreland Cargo. He was the principal of the Mount Washington school system, but he suffered a stroke in 1911 in an office of the school and later died. Whittier School began in 1899. St. Mary of the Mount High School had its first graduation class in 1912, and South Hills High School had its first class commencement in 1917.

Formally dressed, the class of 1906 from Cargo School sits on the steps of the school. The young men wore jackets and ties and the girls' dresses were to the ankle. How times have changed. (Courtesy of Lois Knell.)

This photograph shows students all dressed up for their seventh grade class picture in 1938. It was taken in front of Boggs School. Lois Knell is third from the left in the third row. Knell grew up to be an owner of Knell's Bakery together with her husband. In addition, she is a fine organist and still plays at the Grandview United Presbyterian Church. (Courtesy of Lois Knell.)

This group of smiling sixth graders poses for their class picture on the steps of Whittier School. Note the boys' belted jackets and knickers. Most of the girls have the same hairdo. The date of the photograph is not known.

This happy looking group of children from the seventh and eighth grades of St. Mary of the Mount High School pose for their yearly class picture. In the third row, second from left, is Donald Wuerl, who later became the bishop of Pittsburgh, and the archbishop of Washington, D.C. His sister Carol is third from the right in the first row. (Courtesy of St. Mary of the Mount Alumni Association.)

Students and teachers from Prospect Elementary and Junior High school attend the morning flag rising in 1972. Located at Prospect and Cowan Streets, it took its name from its location. The original building was erected in 1871, but was destroyed by fire in 1914. In 1938, a new building was erected. Designed by James T. Steen, it was constructed of cream brick with limestone and terra-cotta trim. It was considered a monument to Prof. Robert Moreland Cargo. (Courtesy of Library and Archives Division, Historical Society of Western Pennsylvania, Pittsburgh.)

Children file into Whittier School in September 1948. Whittier School honors Isaac Whittier, a director in Mount Washington schools and a burgess of that district before it was annexed to the City of Pittsburgh in 1872. Whittier came to Pittsburgh and took charge of the first classes in the East Ward. The first Whittier School was in existence from 1889 to 1939 and was located at Meridan and Pawnee Streets. A new school designed by M. M. Sheen opened at 150 Meridan Street in 1939. (Courtesy of Library and Archives Division, Historical Society of Western Pennsylvania, Pittsburgh.)

Cargo School was erected in 1896. It was named in honor of Prof. Robert M. Cargo who was the supervising principal of the Mount Washington schools for 43 years. Cargo had a stroke on August 16, 1911, in an office of Prospect school and died the next day. (Courtesy of Library and Archives Division, Historical Society of Western Pennsylvania, Pittsburgh.)

These youngsters attended St. Mary of the Mount Elementary School. The photograph was taken by local photographer John Peden. His daughter is second from the left in the first row. The nun is from the order of the Immaculate Heart of Mary, the order that still serves St. Mary's. (Courtesy of St. Mary of the Mount Alumni Association.)

Typewriters may be a thing of the past, but typing was still very popular and useful in the 1950s when this class of South Hills High School students was pictured. Both boys and girls signed up to take commercial courses. South Hills High School (SHHS) occupied a whole city block. It served students from Beechview, Brookline, and Mount Washington. In addition, it served Catholic students from St. Catherine's, Resurrection, and St. Henry's. (Courtesy of Library and Archives Division, Historical Society of Western Pennsylvania, Pittsburgh.)

South Hills High School is located on a full city block bounded by Ruth, Secane, Harwood, and Eureka Streets. It was originally planned as the Bailey High School in 1915. The original wing on Ruth Street was opened on April 7, 1917, with 225 students in the 9th and 10th grades. Pittsburgh architects Alden and Harlow designed this large brown brick and stone building. Though closed in 1986, the school has an active alumni association whose motto is Gone but Not Forgotten. Notable graduates are Congressman James Fulton and opera singer Julius Huehn. (Courtesy of David Vater.)

A father points out to his children the construction undergirdings of the new St. Mary of the Mount High School on January 26, 1956. The building was one of the first steps in the renaissance of Mount Washington, which was part of the redevelopment program of Pittsburgh.

The graduates of the St. Mary of the Mount High School class of 1915 were Margaret Blum, Winifred Cummins, Camilla DiRenna, Anna Doyle, John Ferrick, Ernestine Gearing, Genevieve Gearing, William Geis, John Ginnevan, Earle Haney, Hazel Hall, Grace Hensel, Richard Keaney, Rose Kelly, Catherine Kilcullen, Jane Kilcullen, Andrew King, Paul O'Brien, Mary Powers, Lambert Rectenwald, Margaret Reilly, Felix Rodgers, Gerald Schroth, Frances Schwabedissen, Joseph Stoernell, Margaret Streily, Florence Sullivan, Josephine Sughrue, John Tunney, Dorothy Walther, and Buherworth Welsh. Pictured here are 16 of the graduates, only two of which are identified as Hazel Hall and Gerald Schroth. Andrew King and Gerald Schroth both became priests, and Helen Sullivan became a nun. (Courtesy of St. Mary of the Mount Alumni Association.)

Newly constructed Boggs Avenue School was built in 1928 near the bottom of Boggs Avenue. Architect Sydney F. Heckert designed the elementary school. Old maps show that this property once belonged to J. A. Schuck and later to Margaret Wilbert. Many residents of the mount fondly remember the school. The building was placed on the National Register of Historic Places in 1987.

Pictured is St. Justin Elementary School on Boggs Avenue. This building initially housed Cargo School, but was sold by the city in 1943. It was bought by the Catholic Diocese for $9,000 and was named St. Justin School. It has since closed and is now Justin Plaza Senior Citizen apartments. (Courtesy of Cel Mazzarini.)

This picture titled *A Library is a True Fairyland* is of a group of children of all nationalities. Taken on January 14, 1927, the unidentified children crowd into a group to have their picture taken while attending a "Story Hour for all Nationalities" at Washington Park. (Courtesy of Pittsburgh City Photographer Collection, Archives Service Center, University of Pittsburgh.)

Frank Briganti of Chess Street returned to Pittsburgh in 1986 to revisit old haunts. He reminisced about the library on Grandview Avenue. He said that it was a bottomless delight for him and one of his greatest sources of happiness. For years, every two weeks he made the two-mile trek to get an armful of books. He opined that many children on the mount attended schools with impoverished libraries. He saw the Carnegie Library System as prime mental nourishment for generations of children. (Courtesy of Frank Briganti.)

This 1938 photograph shows the addition to Prospect School. Over the years, Prospect was a junior high school, a middle school, and a grade school. Part of the land, which the school now occupies, was the old Minsinger quarry, brickyard, livery stable, and a 21-room mansion. Fort McKnight was built on this site along with many other redoubts and batteries during the Civil War. In fact, one of the streets on school property was called Fort Street. Mount Washington School was the first school on this site, built in 1871. Its name was later changed to Prospect School and the building was demolished in 1931 to make way for a new building.

It was 1971 and the Acquariums, a South Hills High School singing group met at WTAE-TV to videotape their entry into Joe Negri's High School Talent Scene. Joe Negri is seen here talking to the group's music teacher, Neal Huguley, of Knoxville Junior High School. (Courtesy of Library and Archives Division, Historical Society of Western Pennsylvania, Pittsburgh.)

82

The class of 1944 from St. Justin High School gets together at a reunion in 1954. Pictured are, from left to right, (first row) John Krigger, Catherine Sportolari, Anna Mae O'Toole, Jean Schaffer, Ruth Humble, Virginia Toomey, and Guy Galasso; (second row) Rita Zeker, Jean Frief, Mary Louise Creehan, Anna Marie McGroder, Hermine Pellegrini, Rose Marie Shenkel, Edith Galasso, and Bernard Pizzaferri; (third row) Jack Steele, Dolores Schoedel, Janet Dowd, Ann Marie Miller, Isabel Dabecco, Margaret Scanlon, and Mary Jane Santa; (fourth row) Leonard Unitas, Harry Marks, Leonard Morgan, Robert Ging, and Anthony Fortunato. (Courtesy of William Galasso.)

The St. Justin High School graduating class of 1944 had their pictures taken in their caps and gowns. Though many of the graduates are from Mount Washington and Duquesne Heights, others are from Brookline, Beechview, and other South Hills neighborhoods. (Courtesy of Hermine Pellegrini Butch.)

The class of 1946 from St. Mary of the Mount High School attends a luncheon. Not all can be identified. On the right is Jerome Schwertz, and beside him is Sally Hirleman. Schwertz lived on Amabel Street for a short time and later moved in with his aunt Hazel Hall Schroth at 116 Merrimac Street after his father's death. Schroth was pictured in the graduation class of 1915.

Mardi Gras is celebrated each year before the start of lent. At St. Justin High School, a Mardi Gras queen and king were selected by the students in the junior and senior classes. The year of this picture was 1945. The queen was Eileen Burge and the king was Lindy Adams. Their attendants were, from left to right, Patricia O'Donnell, Mary Clark, Jane Keast, Janet Martin, Anna Marie Leslie, Thelma Fallert, Peg Scanlon, Harry Conroy, Jack Clark, Jack Philbin, Donald Thompson, Richard Diamond, Robert Laneve, and Richard Moore. (Courtesy of Janet Martin Fagan.)

This picture includes students from St. Justin High School classes of 1946 and 1947. The Mardi Gras queen is Janet Martin and the king is Donald Thompson. Their attendants are, from left to right, (first row) unidentified, unidentified, Dolores Henry, unidentified, Dick Bordone, and unidentified; (second row) Rose Marie Brown, Norma Burge, Marcella Martin, unidentified, unidentified, Catherine Lee, Thomas Horan, Joe Stubenbort, Eugene Rogers, and Philip Fagan (who later married the queen). Although World War II was winding down at their graduations, several of the pictured young men later served in the military. (Courtesy of Janet Martin Fagan.)

St. Justin High School's class of 1946 poses with one of their teachers, who is the nun pictured in the middle of the first row. All were thrilled that she could attend. Mercy nuns taught at St. Justin's, both at the elementary and at the high school. (Courtesy of Janet Martin Fagan.)

The class of 1947 from St. Justin High School poses for a picture. Only 32 out of a class of 82 were able to attend this reunion at the school. Women's hats were still fashionable for special occasions in 1954. (Courtesy of Nancy Kimmerle.)

The class of 1946 attends a reunion of St. Justin High School in 1996. Photographer John Peden from Mount Washington photographed each class. The students are, from left to right, (first row) Janet Martin, Jane Whiteside, Nancy Strauss, Audrey Weiss, Mary Ann Crowe, Mary Rose, and Florence Falkenhagen; (second row) Mary Lynch, Rose Marie D'Allesandro, Rose Mary Walsh, and Dolores Brown; (third row) Jerome Madden, Joe Stubenbort, Paul Leslie, unidentified, Thomas Horan, Bruno Tambellini, Paul Demmer, Paul Farrell, Regis Landy, Gene Yost, Robert Lawrence, and Stanley Balcer. (Courtesy of Janet Martin Fagan.)

The class of 1947 attends their school reunion 23 years after graduation, in 1970. This year no hats are visible on the women, and hair is a little scarcer on the men. Though only 41 out of 82 attended, there were more at this reunion than at the last. The class was assured that all were well but were unable to attend.

The class of 1951 attends a St. Justin High School reunion in 1976. William Galasso is in the third row on the far left. John Unitas is the tallest man in the third row. The others are not identified. Galasso has lived at 428 Boggs Avenue for over 60 years in the house that his father, Benjamin, bought. Unitas played football for St. Justin High School and eventually for the Baltimore Colts and the San Diego Chargers. In 1969, during a celebration to mark the National Football League's 50th anniversary, Unitas was named "the greatest quarterback of all time." (Courtesy of William Galasso.)

The 1947 graduation class from St. Justin High School gathers at their 50th reunion. From left to right are (first row) Marcella Martin Link, Bill O'Connor, and Margie Schafer; (second row) Bob Schafer, Dick Moore, his wife Loretta, John Manzione, his unidentified wife, Yvonne O'Connor, Phil Fagan, Janet Martin Fagan, Alice Kirschner Sinesky, Nancy Kimmerle Beck, Mickey Ehland Stitt, Joe Daube, and Eddie Shaffer.

James Jamison holds a sign in 1979. Parents protested to stop busing neighborhood children to other schools in the city. Their efforts were unsuccessful and today all city students are bused to schools not in their own neighborhoods. Prospect was turned into a middle school and later became both a middle school and an elementary school. It was closed in 2006. (Courtesy of Cel Mazzarini.)

St. Mary of the Mount High School, pictured in the process of being torn down, was demolished so that apartments could be built on the site. Located on Grandview Avenue, it was across the street from the elementary school. The high school was created in 1910 with the first class graduating in 1912. The last class graduated in 1982. (Courtesy of Cel Mazzarini.)

During the Civil War, a battery was a simple defensive work for a six-gun artillery unit of men and cannon. This wooded area hardly seems likely to have been a battery. However, during the beginnings of the Civil War, it was. Located in a lot near Fingal Street, it was one of several built in that area by cautious Pittsburghers ready to defend if need be. Another battery named Fort Mechanic was located on a crest behind a building at 122 Bailey Avenue. This completed fort on June 27, 1863, was the scene of a public gathering and flag-raising. Needless to say, the defenses were not used.

These four young ladies attended high school at St. Justin's on Lelia Street. They are dressed for a Halloween party at a skating rink honoring veterans of World War II. Seen here, from left to right, Alice Kirschner wears a cheerleader's sweater from St. Justin; Ruth Ford wears a Navy outfit; Betty Hurney a Navy officer's outfit; and Nancy Kimmerle the Marine outfit from her returned cousin who served in Saipan and Guadel Canal. The girls were to graduate in 1947.

William Street is a steep, narrow, and curvy road that runs from Boggs and Bailey Avenues to Arlington Avenue, near the Liberty Tubes. This house on William Street was badly damaged in a fire. It was rumored that the Unitas family once lived here. (Courtesy of Michael J. Liss.)

Seven

Sports and Other Pastimes

Mount Washington and Duquesne Heights people have always been sports-minded. Baseball was the most popular sport in the summer. The Old Church League was the best-known team. Formed in 1906, it disbanded just before the beginning of World War I. The *Mount Washington News* reported in 1954 that old-timers agreed that the teams of the day could not begin to measure up to the teams of the Old Church League in its prime. They believed that some of those players could easily have qualified for the major leagues. Also enjoyed were football, tennis, bowling, roller-skating, and track. Roller-skating was a rough sport and, as played at the Shiloh Rink, was called roller polo. Duckpin bowlers were seen as "the best bowlers who ever laid a ball on the maple lanes" of the Poke Lanes. Imagine a bowling alley above your head. Poke Lanes were on the second floor of Skirboll's Variety Store. Popular also was the basketball team, the Knights of King Arthur, known as KOKA. They won the championship of the Washington Heights League in 1920.

Women were not to be denied the challenge and pleasure of team sports. The Polar Maids played hockey in 1916 and the Bloomer Girls from Ohio were defeated eight to three by the Mount Washington women's group, the Independents. The Mount Washington Lyceum girls who won the city championship in 1913 played basketball as early as 1910. In 1909, John Gillespie, the baseball league president, hoped that there could be a Catholic team to compete in the league. That year St. Mary of the Mount Catholic Church joined the league and won the pennant. On September 11, 1910, the mayor of Pittsburgh, William A. Magee, dedicated the first community gymnasium. High school teams of basketball and football were formed later, with teams from St. Justin High School, St. Mary of the Mount High School, and South Hills High School having winning seasons. Enthusiastic students cheered them on, led by cheerleaders.

Four young men from the class of 1947 show support for their school holding the banner of St. Justin's. Pictured are, from left to right, (first row) Robert Schafer and Edward Shaffer; (second row) James McConville and Norman Winterhalter. They are pictured in the front of James McConville's home in Beechview. (Courtesy of James McConville.)

In the 1940s, football was as big as it is now in Pittsburgh. Catholic schools were very competitive and dedicated to their teams. These young fellows practiced on natural turf, in some semblance of a uniform. They were loved and cheered by their classmates. A few of the players are identified as Dick Bordone, Sil Ferrari, Jack Graner, and Phil Fagan. (Courtesy of Philip Fagan.)

Where would the players be without the cheerleaders? Enthusiastic and athletic cheerleaders led cheers for the football and basketball games at St. Justin High School in the late 1940s. Shown are, from left to right, (first row) Dolores Henry, Lois White, and Patricia O'Donnell; (second row) Dorothy Ginley, Marcella Martin, Lois Leitholf, and Margaret Mary Ehland. In the 1950s, cheerleaders were unknowingly fortunate enough to cheer for a football player who later achieved national fame, John Unitas. In 1956 he joined the Baltimore Colts team, becoming the team's star quarterback. During his 18-year career, he played in 10 Pro Bowls, and was the first quarterback to throw for 40,000 yards. In 1969, he was inducted into the Pro Football Hall of Fame.

The white shirts are from St. Justin High School and the dark shirts from St. Luke High School. The player with No. 42 on his shirt, flying through the air over a St. Luke's player, is Philip Fagan. He claims that he was trying to block a kick. Number 40 is Jack Ziefel. In 1946, when this photograph was taken, Catholic schools were very competitive in football and basketball. Their schools' athletic associations purchased their uniforms. Take note of the old helmets. (Courtesy of Philip Fagan.)

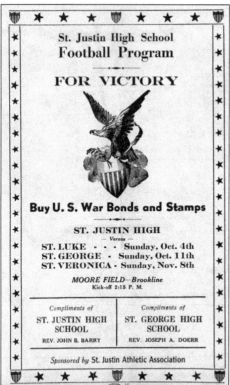

St. Justin High School
Football Program

FOR VICTORY

Buy U. S. War Bonds and Stamps

ST. JUSTIN HIGH
— Versus —
ST. LUKE · · · Sunday, Oct. 4th
ST. GEORGE · Sunday, Oct. 11th
ST. VERONICA · Sunday, Nov. 8th

MOORE FIELD—Brookline
Kick-off 2:15 P. M.

Compliments of | *Compliments of*
ST. JUSTIN HIGH SCHOOL | ST. GEORGE HIGH SCHOOL
REV. JOHN B. BARRY | REV. JOSEPH A. DOERR

Sponsored by St. Justin Athletic Association

The St. Justin Athletic Association printed the programs for football playoffs. Football in Pittsburgh high schools was popular in the 1940s even though the nation was involved in a great war. Patriotism was high and everyone was urged to buy U.S. war bonds and war stamps. Many of the young men who participated in this football program were soon off to war. (Courtesy of Philip Fagan.)

The St. Justin High School basketball team poses for their picture in 1946 on the steps of the school, flanked by their student manager Rich Cunningham (left) and their coach J. McDermott (right). The players are, from left to right (first row) Dick Bordone, Richard Diamond, Dario Icardi, Jack White, Jack Graner, and ? Maffey; (second row) John Manzione, Paul Leslie, Thomas Horan, Donald Thompson, Paul Demmer, and Raymond Castello. The basketball team was every bit as enthusiastic about their game as were the football team. Note that many of the same boys were on both teams. It makes one wonder how they fit schoolwork into their busy schedules. Yet they did and proved to be successful at both.

Frank Gracey, No. 26, and Ron Sanders, No. 47, practice kicking for an upcoming game. The St. Mary of the Mount High School football program was discontinued when the war started and did not continue until 1947. One of their first games was with St. Justin High School. A member of St. Justin's team remembers that there was a large crowd seen at Moore field where the game was played. People were on the hillside and on the field, and the game was delayed until the field could be cleared. (Courtesy of St. Mary of the Mount Alumni Office.)

Here are the girls that led the cheers for St. Mary of the Mount High School teams. In this picture the Great Big Mounties Cheerleaders do acrobatic cheers for a game of basketball. From the scoreboard it appears that the home team was winning by a score of 30 to 20. (Courtesy of St. Mary of the Mount Alumni Office.)

Adults may also enjoy sports. Perhaps a little less strenuous, but these men enjoy the sport of duckpins, which was popular in the 1940s. Taken at Chez Dee's supper club in 1962, are the members of St. Justin Catholic War Veterans Duckpin Bowling League. (Courtesy of William Galasso.)

The first place winning team of the Catholic War Veterans Bowling League in 1991 celebrate their victory. Pictured are, from left to right, Vic Cristofenelli, Michael Stypula, Richard Frohman, Guy Galasso, Ray Weslager, and Joe Grimes. (Courtesy of William Galasso.)

Here is the 1947–1948 Washington Heights boys' basketball team. From left to right are (first row) Richard Walsh; (second row) Beau Reed, Robert Rawsthorne, and Larry Lightheisen; (third row) Clarence Rall, Charles Thomas, Robert Thomas, Paul Walsh, Ralph Shipley, and coach Paul Walsh.

Girls from the Mount Washington and Duquesne Heights area won the Washington Heights Athletic Association Slo-Pitch Championship. Seen here in July 2003, they get ready to play at PNC Park with the city in the background. (Courtesy of Cel Mazzarini.)

In 1963, Paul Manion created and managed the JFK football league. Called "Meatball" by all who knew and loved him, he was also responsible for the basketball and hockey leagues. He instituted a youth honor guard that marched at funerals and in parades. He was known to Mount Washingtonians as an avid, dedicated leader of activities for young people. In this photograph, he is awarded at a special ceremony where he was recognized for his contributions to the youth of the area. His caricature is on the wall behind him. A shelter is named after him in Olympia Park in honor of his contributions. (Courtesy of Cel Mazzarini.)

When football at St. Mary of the Mount High School was reinstituted after the war in 1947, junior high boys were also able to form a team. This squad of boys posed in 1948 with full uniforms. (Courtesy of St. Mary of the Mount Alumni Office.)

With South Hills High School in the background, a crowd of people gathers by the path during a meet in Washington Park on August 26, 1921. (Courtesy of the Pittsburgh City Photographer Collection, Archives Service Center, University of Pittsburgh.)

This popular swimming recreation area was a delight for many children and adults. It entertained by holding water carnivals with fancy diving, novelty races, and clown acts. Ream Pool is located on the corner of Merrimac Street and Virginia Avenue. (Courtesy of Library and Archives Division, Historical Society of Western Pennsylvania, Pittsburgh.)

In the 1940s, the Pittsburgh Parks and Recreation Department hired college students to work in the city parks to maintain order, help with recreation, and teach neighborhood children during the summer months. Mary Jane Kimmerle was hired to serve at Arlington Playground for two summers and at Olympia Park for two summers while she attended the University of Pittsburgh. Olympia Park was dedicated in 1907, and had been in constant use for over 40 years. (Courtesy of Mary Jane Kimmerle Schwertz.)

People throng around the Haven Heights United Methodist Church for its annual Easter Egg Hunt in April 2006. This is one of many activities offered by Haven Heights Church. (Courtesy of Haven Heights United Methodist Church.)

In September 2004, a gentleman brings his little dog to be blessed, on the annual blessing of the animals at Haven Heights Church. (Courtesy of Haven Heights United Methodist Church.)

This photograph shows the latest 1925 swimwear as modeled by George and Mary Boxheimer of 102 Olympia Street in Duquesne Heights. How the styles have changed. (Courtesy of Mary Boxheimer.)

Though seemingly not a pastime, it certainly was for the children. Pittsburgh's big snow of the 1950s left Merrimac Street impassable for hours until the roads were finally cleared. Transportation was delayed for hours leaving many workers finding it difficult, if not impossible to get to work. Cars that had parked on the street were buried, but children found it to be great fun. (Courtesy of Virginia Peden.)

Founded in 1949 and disbanded in 1989, the Women's Club of Mount Washington celebrated Founder's Day in January 1990. Pictured at the podium are Helen Reisdorf and Virginia Peden. The president, Jean Solimbene, stands at the left with Mary Figura, to the right. The women's club brought people together from all areas. They contributed to many causes and supported community events. (Courtesy of Virginia Peden.)

The Grandview, the Shiloh, and the Glade Theaters provided entertainment for many years. *Love Me Tender* headlined Elvis Presley, showing on Monday and Tuesday only. The usual cost was 5¢ for children and 10¢ for adults. Skirboll's Gift Shop occupied the space that once was the Shiloh. It is now a State Store. Another theater, the Lyric, operated by Harry Reiff, was located at 21 Boggs Avenue. It had 190 seats and was sometimes referred to as "Idle-a-while." (Courtesy of Cel Mazzarini.)

THE OLD LYRIC THEATER at 21 Boggs Ave. was operated by Harry E. Reiff who bought the 190-seat house from Harry Arnold. The latter had named the theater the "Idle-a-While." Mr. Reiff also operated the show on Shiloh St. which now houses The News.

GRANDVIEW

THE SHOW-PLACE OF
MT. WASHINGTON
Phone: HEmlock 1-6344

THURS.-FRI.-SAT.   AUG. 26-27-28
Big Triple Treat Show
NO. 1
Robert Mitchum, Jack Palance
—in—
"SECOND CHANCE"
NO. 2
George Montgomery in
"THE LONE GUN"
NO. 3
THE THREE STOOGES in
"SPOOKS"

SUNDAY-MONDAY   AUG. 29-30
Mickey Spillane's
"THE LONG WAIT"
with Anthony Quinn
—and—
Van Heflin, Wanda Hendrix in
**"THE GOLDEN
MASK"**
IN TECHNICOLOR

TUES.-WED   AUG. 31-SEPT. 1
**17 BIG ALL NEW
CARTOONS**
BUGS BUNNY—TOM & JERRY
DONALD DUCK
2 BIG FULL HOURS OF ALL
YOUR CARTOON FAVORITES

CARTOONS START AT 7 P. M.
Gene Kelly, Debbie Reynolds in
**"SINGIN' IN THE
RAIN"**
IN TECHNICOLOR

COMING—SEPTEMBER
"Apache"
"Gone with the Wind"
"Caine Mutiny"

Mellon National Bank and Trust Co.

14th St. and E. Carson

South Side

•

Member
Federal Deposit Insurance Corporation

This shows the list of movies that were playing at the Grandview Theater in 1954. The page is from the *Mount Washington News* edition of August 10, 1954. It shows a picture of the old Lyric Theater and an advertisement for Mellon National Bank. The bank, a pioneer in the Pittsburgh district, moved some of its banking facilities out of the city. Its main office and branches are now Citizen's Bank.

The Knights of Malta stand in formation in front of the Mount Washington Library. Established in 1914, for years the band was one of the district's most outstanding musical groups. The trombonist (third row, third from right) is Harry Smithyman. Waldo Brooks is the trombone player (third row, third from the left). Chuck Lowman is seen in the second row, fourth from right. The Knights of Malta is a subordinate commandery of the oldest knightly order in existence.

Grandview Avenue has been the site of many festivities, from parades to protests to weddings. Pictured here in 1976, from left to right, are (first row) Herman Knell, his son Keith, and Lois Knell; (second row) sons David and Paul Knell. They were selling tarts from their bakery at a Grandview Avenue Fair for 25¢ each or $1.49 for six. (Courtesy of Lois Knell.)

A movie company filmed a movie in Mount Washington and had to turn Knell's Bakery into Pulaski's just for the picture. They must have admired the fine architecture of the building. This was not the only movie to be made in Mount Washington. *Mrs. Soffel*, starring Diane Keaton and Mel Gibson, was also shot in Pittsburgh and Mount Washington to depict the story of the warden's wife and the Biddle brothers. (Courtesy of Lois Knell.)

Against the backdrop of the buildings in downtown Pittsburgh, workmen build an observation deck on Grandview Avenue on October 24, 1967. The men on the edge looked down on a very steep hill, unprotected by the fence that they would eventually build. (Courtesy of the Pittsburgh City Photographer Collection, Archives Service Center, University of Pittsburgh.)

A music festival at Grandview Park drew a large crowd. Grandview Park consists of 18 acres of land. Sitting on the wall and on the ground was fine because the weather on September 28, 1969, was balmy and clear. (Courtesy of the Pittsburgh City Photographer Collection, Archives Service Center, University of Pittsburgh.)

Skirboll's sold anything that you might want, from shoes to nails. The saying went that if you could not get it at Skirboll's, you could not get it anywhere. Opened in 1900 by Harry and Fannie Skirboll, it began as a dry goods store. Their son Leonard worked there when he was 10 years old, but as a man he went on the road, selling men's wear. When his dad died in 1954, Leonard Skirboll took over the business. Leonard's wife of 44 years, Tamara, opened a gift shop up the street in the space that was once the Shiloh Theater. In 1980, Leonard closed the five-and-dime, sold the space to Thrift Drug, and joined his wife in the gift shop. However, after the Skirboll's were in business for 105 years, their last store, the gift shop, was closed. Leonard is sitting in the Village Dairy that is in the space that once was the Skirboll store. (Courtesy of Leonard Skirboll.)

It was July 1956, and once again, a concert was held at Grandview Park. Many more people were across the street sitting on the hillside. Concerts were held frequently in the park.

From left to right, sisters Catherine Lynch and Margaret Riley were swimming with a friend but stopped long enough to have their picture taken. (Courtesy of Mary Boxheimer.)

Friends of Julia Boxheimer picnicked at Olympia Park. They were having fun enjoying the warm weather. Only one man is in sight. (Courtesy of Mary Boxheimer.)

Pictured here are cheerleaders in babushkas. It must have been raining when they were leading the cheers for St. Justin High School football players who were playing St. George High School. Their wool sweaters are wet and stretched; yet they are still smiling. Pictured are, from left to right, (first row) Janet Martin, Mary Anne Crowe, and Ruth Ann Bieber; (second row) Rosemarie Brown, Alice Adams, and Mary Jane Kimmerle. (Courtesy of Janet Martin Fagan.)

These large, chimney-like structures and the building are the ventilation plant for the Liberty Tubes. The plant is at the bottom of Ruth Street, seemingly not even near the tubes.

A Christmas Eve fire caused this devastation. Formerly a neighborhood saloon on Southern Avenue named Belinski's, it was bought by Ambrogies and made into a fine dining establishment. However, an electrical connection caused the fire to destroy the building. It was torn down and is now an empty lot. (Courtesy of the Mazzarini Family.)

Is this progress? Remember reading about when people had to trudge up the Indian Trail steps? Then yes, this is progress. Two motorcycles are seen parked in front of a store, Eiselltown, which sells lottery tickets and sends faxes—two unknown entities 20 years ago. And how easy it is to push a gas pedal rather than a foot.

This is an example of the houses in Chatham Village. The property on which the village stands was a small part of the land owned by Maj. Abraham Kirkpatrick. It remained in the possession of his descendants until the Buhl Foundation purchased it in 1931.

Eight

AND NOW

And now, today, what is the mount like? What pictures will children and grandchildren save for their children to see? In this book, only a fragment of the past can be illustrated. The history of Mount Washington cannot be told in a few words or by looking at a few pictures. Indeed, this book is but a smattering of the life of this exciting town. Mount Washington and Duquesne Heights have such a vast and complicated story to tell that only a taste of the occurrences are pictured herein. In reality, some of the pictorial history may be gone forever, much like that of its owners. Yet, if it were possible to garner all of the information hidden in albums, in attics, or in basements, this book would be 10 times as large. Unfortunately, the many fine restaurants could be mentioned only briefly, and the tiny family restaurants or bars that are frequented daily had to be passed over. Many of the pioneer families who lived here since the time of Coal Hill are not represented, except in name only. Churches' long histories, though not ignored, were not reported in detail with all of their accomplishments. However, though small and limited, this book presents a picture to those who were not there in years past, so that they may appreciate how their ancestors lived and what they accomplished.

And now, this final chapter presents the mount as it is today. The people are the mount. The old-timers who labored, raised families, went to church, and sent their children to school are still represented in most areas of Mount Washington and Duquesne Heights. Some new residents, and sometimes its old residents, are taking the big old homes and converting them into townhouses and condos. Where once one family lived, now two or three families occupy the same amount of space, made over into modern, well-appointed homes. And so, in all its glory, with all its complications or problems, with all its beauty, a presentation is offered to all. Here is the mount.

The mount would not be the mount without the incline. This beautiful picture is known the nation over and maybe the world over. After all, it was designed and built by early German immigrants, and people of many nations visit it. Even in black and white, it is impressive. Yet it is and was more than a tourist attraction, a beautiful picture, or thrill giver. It provided for generations of people a shorter way from the mount into downtown Pittsburgh than the longer ride on the No. 40 streetcar.

Looks like a giant cogwheel, right? But what is it? Found in the engine room of the incline, on tours of the incline, the engineers demonstrate how the wheel winds up the cable pulling the car up. (Courtesy of David Vater.)

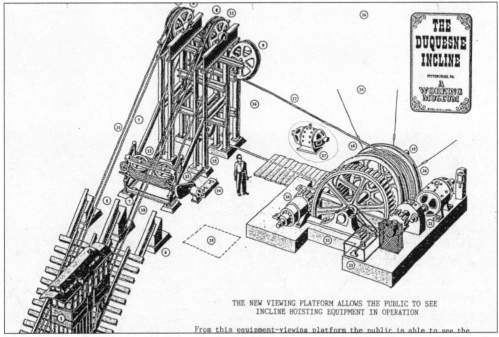

THE NEW VIEWING PLATFORM ALLOWS THE PUBLIC TO SEE
INCLINE HOISTING EQUIPMENT IN OPERATION

From this equipment-viewing platform the public is able to see the

This sketch is from the Incline Museum. It describes the workings of the Duquesne Incline. An interesting part is No. 27 (circled). It is a Navy surplus motor manufactured for use on a United States Navy destroyer, but never installed due to the end of World War II. It was purchased as a back-up unit for the incline.

This sketch is available at the top station of the Duquesne Incline. It depicts the different aspects of the incline. One, on the upper left, is the mechanism of the incline with the wooden-toothed drive gear and cable drum; the footbridge across Carson Street is at the lower left; the incline itself with the inset of a car on the lower right; and finally, the Point, the city and the rivers at top right. This 1984 sketch is by Edward Dumont.

The Monongahela Incline takes passengers to Grandview Avenue on its way up and to Carson Street on its way down. It only goes six miles per hour, but that gives more time to marvel at the view, or, if going to work, to read the paper.

Two young first-time riders turn from the view to have their picture taken with the city in the background. (Courtesy of Harrison Beck.)

What fun it is to ride the incline up to Grandview Avenue. Sometimes, people ride just to take the grandchildren to see their expressions—sometimes fear, sometimes excitement. Sometimes people ride to dine at one of the fine restaurants that dot the landscape along Grandview Avenue. Sometimes people ride only to marvel at the view. The Duquesne Heights Incline closely follows the tracks of one of the old coal hoists. Built by Samuel Dreischer, a German immigrant and engineer, it opened on May 20, 1877. It was the first one built by Dreischer, who eventually built 17 additional inclines in the city. In 1880, *Scientific American* noted that "on Sundays during the summer 6,000 passengers are carried during the day and evening." Pictured are two young tourists from Florida. After a ride up, they stood on the overlook to view the city and the river, with the pleasure boats docked below. (Courtesy of Hayley N. Beck.)

The overlook was recently reconditioned because Pittsburgh was holding the All-Star game of 2005, and many tourists were expected. Standing on the platform and viewing the city are a group of Asian men. (Courtesy of Mount Washington Community Development Corporation.)

This photograph will go back to Japan or Korea. That can give Mount Washingtonians bragging rights, because this spot is a must for visitors to the city, whether from Asia or East Podunk. (Courtesy of Mount Washington Community Development Corporation.)

This picture is another reason why tourists visit Mount Washington. Diners at the Georgetown Inn on Grandview Avenue are enjoying a good meal while celebrating a special occasion. The restaurants on Grandview Avenue attract residents and tourists. The Lamont, the Tin Angel, Monterey Bay, the Georgetown Inn, and Bella Vista all have delicious food and offer an absolutely amazing sight. When the Pittsburgh Pirates play, there are fireworks.

There is more to Mount Washington than the view. There are the people. Leonard Skirboll exclaimed that he loves the mount, even though he had to move to the east end for health reasons. He still returns to the Village Dairy for breakfast. It is a clean middle-class neighborhood of working people. People who work in town find it easy to take the incline to Carson Street and walk across the bridge to town, or to catch a bus or trolley to other sections of the city. Good restaurants are within walking distance, as well as banks, grocery stores and diners.

This is the view of the downtown area of the city of Pittsburgh that tourists see. This picture was taken from the ship the *Majestic*, which tours the three rivers of Pittsburgh. The tall dark building is the U.S. Steel Building. The building off center with the four pointed turrets is the Pittsburgh Plate Glass building. Pittsburgh has several pleasure boats that offer entertainment and dancing as well as a ride on the rivers.

Pictured is a fragment of the back slopes of Mount Washington. They are not as precipitous as the front slopes that face the Monongahela River. This picture was taken from the 10th floor of St. Justin Plaza on Boggs Avenue. (Courtesy of Michael Liss.)

As one walks along Grandview Avenue, one will see this sign placed by the Pennsylvania Historical and Museum Commission. It is a reminder that men and women labored on this hill in the dust and harsh conditions. Not only was the labor difficult, but for a time in the late 1700s, the Native Americans were still hostile to the newcomers.

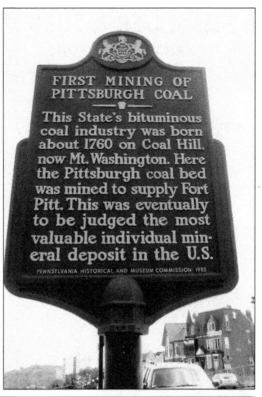

This plaque commemorating Verna Dibble's very large contribution to the beautification of the hillside is on the fence along Grandview Avenue across from St. Mary of the Mount Catholic Church. Her daughters have collected many albums with correspondence to various organizations and government officials concerning the beautification of the hill. They included not only planting on the hill, but also her efforts to have unsightly advertising signs removed.

Slater's has served the community for over 100 years. Wm. Slater and Sons, established in 1881, is among the oldest undertaking firms in the city of Pittsburgh. William Slater came to this country from Westphalia, Germany, in 1867, and to Mount Washington in 1873. Slater was an industrious man running an undertaking establishment and a grocery store without help until 1891, when his eldest son, John, stepped in to help. Three more of his sons, Harry, Fred, and Raymond, joined them in a few years. His daughter Ida also stepped in with administrative duties. She remembered that funerals in those days were not held from a funeral home, but in a church. In 1918, modernization established that funerals could be from the funeral home. William died in 1932, and two of his children and later generations carried on with the business.

This 1959 painting by H. F. Tracey hangs in the Mount Washington Carnegie Library. It is a rendering of the land around 1886 as the painter pictured it from his research. The area was more rural then and there were many springs along the hillsides, most of which were drained or rerouted due to the mines, rapacious development, and paving of streets. Note the stream below East Sycamore Street. It is gone now, but it lives on in Tracey's painting, a reminder of the natural beauty of our mount. The painting is in the downstairs of the library. It is worth going down to see it. (Courtesy of Michael Liss.)

Riders on the incline can take a picture like this. A resident recently took this fascinating view of Pittsburgh's Point. (Courtesy of the Mount Washington Community Development Corporation.)

Taken on a chilly, windy day in October, the fountain at the Point had pink water to remind people about breast cancer precautions. The picture was taken around Sweetbriar Street in Duquesne Heights.

Two couples walk along Grandview Avenue. Taken from near the overlook, they must be residents because one girl has a number seven shirt on, Ben Roethlisberger's number. He is the young quarterback for the Pittsburgh Steelers.

With the mount in the background, the fountain at the Point rises high. The water for the fountain comes from Pittsburgh's fourth river. It is little known, but is an underground river and it supplies the water for the fountain year-round, or whenever the weather allows.

Taken from Duquesne Heights, this view of the city shows the USX Tower (the tall dark building), and the Highmark Building with the pointed roof. The Monongahela River is barely seen under the bridge. Since Pittsburgh has three rivers, it is rare to get anywhere without crossing a bridge.

As seen from Mount Washington, the factories and homes of the South Side blend together into one large conglomeration. The Birmingham Bridge, painted green, is in the distance. (Courtesy of Michael Liss.)

This impressive statue was sculpted by James West and donated to the city of Pittsburgh. Pictured across from one of the well-known restaurants in Duquesne Heights is the statue of George Washington conversing with the great Seneca chief Guyasuta. The statue was unveiled on October 25, 2006.

James West (left), the designer and sculptor of the statue, poses with the mayor of the city of Pittsburgh, Luke Ravenstahl, and his model for Guyasuta, Paul Winney, a Seneca Indian from a reservation in New York State.

This view of the statue has a background of the city. The statue was placed on rocks built and placed by the city's Public Works Department. The statue is named *A Point of View* and the area where it lies is now called the Point of View Park. It will be a part of the Scenic Byways Park.

Attending the unveiling of the statue were several Native Americans, most of whom were of the Seneca tribe. The Senecas belonged to the Six Nations of Indians, which included among others, the Shawnee, the Delaware, Wyandots, and Mingos. They were hostile to the settlers in and around Fort Pitt, siding first with the French, and later, with the British. It was in October 1770 that Washington met with Guyasuta, seeking a treaty. This pictured Native American was Seneca, coming to Pittsburgh from Ohio.

Reenactors attended the unveiling of the statue giving a realistic theme for the event. There were six frontiersman dressed in pioneer attire with muskets and powder horns. Ordered by a militiaman in a British red uniform, they shot their muskets toward Fort Pitt.

Only one woman in frontier attire attended the ceremony. Clothing was very difficult to attain around Fort Pitt in those early days. There were no stores or peddlers, and clothes had to last for years, through rain, hard work, and Native American raids. She was drinking from an earthenware jug. That must have been a luxury because dishes and utensils were rare. She laughingly assured that the jug was authentic.

It is with great pride that the people of Mount Washington and, indeed, the entire city of Pittsburgh, acknowledge the appointment of Donald Wuerl to be the archbishop of Washington, D.C. Born on November 12, 1940, he attended St. Mary of the Mount Elementary School and High School. He attended Georgetown University, the Gregorian University of Rome, and the University of St. Thomas in Rome where he received a doctorate in 1974. He became a priest on December 17, 1966, and was named bishop on February 12, 1988. The motto on his Coat of Arms is Thy Kingdom Come.

Greetings from Pittsburgh

The view of Pittsburgh at night is spectacular. A resident whose living room and bedroom face the city claims that the lights at night have a calming effect. Postcards such as this must have been mailed to every country in the world.

Visit us at
arcadiapublishing.com

9 781531 630805